D0041783

FLIPPING
BURGERS
TO FLIPPING
MILLIONS

FLIPPING BURGERS

TO FLIPPING

MILLIONS

**A Guide to Financial Freedom Whether
You Have Your Dream Job, Own Your Own
Business, or Just Started Your First Job**

Bernard Kelly

HYPERION

NEW YORK

This book is not designed to be a definitive investment guide or to take the place of advice from a qualified financial planner or other professional. Given the risk involved in investing of almost any kind, there is no guarantee that the investment methods in this book will be profitable. The publisher and author disclaim liability for any losses that may be sustained as a result of applying the methods suggested in the book.

Copyright © 2011 Bernard Kelly

Library of Congress Cataloging-in-Publication Data has been applied for.

ISBN 978-1-4013-2420-9

Hyperion books are available for special promotions and premiums. For details contact the HarperCollins Special Markets Department in the New York office at 212-207-7528, fax 212-207-7222, or e-mail spsales@harpercollins.com.

Book design by Renato Stanisic

FIRST EDITION

10 9 8 7 6 5 4 3 2 1

SUSTAINABLE FORESTRY INITIATIVE
Certified Fiber Sourcing
www.sfiprogram.org

THIS LABEL APPLIES TO TEXT STOCK

We try to produce the most beautiful books possible, and we are also extremely concerned about the impact of our manufacturing process on the forests of the world and the environment as a whole. Accordingly, we made sure that all of the paper we used has been certified as coming from forests that are managed to ensure the protection of the people and wildlife dependent upon them.

To my mother. You have made all I have enjoyed and achieved in this life possible. There have been good times and bad times, exhilarating successes and disheartening failures, but through it all you have been there to encourage and support me. I am forever grateful.

Contents

Throughout the book, I provide hypothetical scenarios that illustrate my basic premise that saving early and consistently can lead to better results over time. For many of these examples, I assume a certain rate of return of ten percent on your invested money. Please note that a ten percent rate of return is made for purposes of example only. No specific rate of return can be guaranteed due to fluctuations in market conditions and your investment choices. Accordingly, you should always seek the advice of a professional financial adviser who is qualified to advise you on the best ways to invest and make the most of the money you've worked so hard to save. However, that does not change the fact that developing financial discipline is crucial to financial success, and this book strives to give you the inspiration and confidence to make positive changes in your financial life.

FLIPPING
BURGERS
TO FLIPPING
MILLIONS

CHAPTER ONE

FLIPPING BURGERS

L et's be clear, I don't own a string of McDonald's stores. I don't even own one. Plenty of people have made millions by owning and operating a business, but this book is not about that. Thirteen years ago, straight out of high school, I took a job working for McDonald's. This book is about how you can become financially free, even if you work at McDonald's.

Today, I am thirty years old. The average net worth of a thirty-year-old in the United States is $73,500. This number is distorted of course by those who have inherited millions from their parents or grandparents. The median net worth for a thirty-year-old is $14,200.

My net worth today is more than thirty times the median net worth of my peers. Now, that may not seem like an enormous amount of money, but by the time you get halfway through the next chapter you will understand why that is an incredible fortune.

It is also important to point out that I have accumulated these investable assets while working for McDonald's. I've never had a second job on the side, I have not inherited a single dollar, and I have not won any money in the lottery. I did lose $40,000 in a bad property investment, but that was a valuable learning experience. What I have done is work hard at my job, using the system I am going to lay out for you in this book.

You may be tempted to say, "Well, Bernard Kelly is special." That would be a mistake. You may be tempted to say, "Things must have come easy for him." That would also be a mistake. Nothing has come easy for me in life. Things just seemed to come easily for many of my friends and for many of my brothers—but not for me.

I failed high school. Miserably. In fact, when I left high school at the end of my senior year I could not read or spell. To say that school was not my thing would be the understatement of the century. But, surprisingly, I liked going to school and I went every day. I wasn't academically gifted, but I have always liked being around people and loved the social aspect of being at school.

Looking back on my years in school, failing class after class, I now realize that I was developing the character necessary for future success. It is difficult and uncomfortable to sit in class and not be able to follow along with the teacher and your classmates. Our natural instinct is to avoid difficult and uncomfortable situations. But it was school, and I had to go. So I learned to adapt and I never stopped trying. These two qualities have been at the center of any success I have enjoyed ever since.

When I left school, I didn't really know what I wanted to do for the rest of my life. All I knew was that I wanted to go to Europe. The only reason I went to work for McDonald's in the first place was because I wanted money to go to Europe. I told myself, "Just do it for three months, save your money, and then you can get out of here and enjoy yourself!"

The first day the store manager put me on fries. I cooked fries all day, every day, for a week. At night I would go home and my wrists would be throbbing in pain. But I stuck at it. The next week I was flipping burgers.

As the weeks passed, I gradually became fascinated with all things McDonald's. I started learning about the history of the company and studying what made a store successful.

I still remember the day I first discovered that McDonald's was my thing. I was cooking burgers when a group of executives from corporate came into the store, wearing their suits and ties, and I thought to myself, "I could do what they do. I could be good at what they do. This is something I can really succeed at."

The day you can say to yourself, "This is my thing," is a great day.

My dream of going to Europe was on the back burner now. I wasn't looking to delay the beginning of my adult life anymore. I was ready to immerse myself in it—and that was a fabulous feeling.

So I taught myself to read, asked a lot of questions of anyone in the business who would take the time to answer, and became an observer of the people, systems, and processes that made up the McDonald's world.

It wasn't long before my passion was recognized. Passion stands out in any environment, but the more mundane the environment or job, the more passion stands out. I worked hard and produced measureable results. I was promoted over and over again. By the time I was twenty-five, I was a store manager, and throughout the process the McDonald's Corporation was educating me. I attended every course that was offered. I was hungry to learn everything I could about the business, and to grow as a person.

Today, I am an operations consultant for the McDonald's Corporation. I oversee six stores, with 38 managers, 420 crew persons, and annual sales of more than $24 million.

McDonald's was my first job and has been my only full-time job. Is it the most glamorous job in the world? No. But it is *my* thing. I am good at it, I enjoy it, and there are an awful lot of people who live their whole lives and can never say that about their work. So I feel incredibly fortunate to have found work that I can enjoy and succeed in at such a young age.

It is perhaps needless to say, but over the years a great many people have put me down and looked down on me because I work at McDonald's. This is one of the universal negative stereotypes of our age. But consider the facts for a moment. . . .

- McDonald's is one of the most ingenious business systems of all time. It has been studied and copied time and time again and is the founding father of both the franchise concept and the chain store concept that are now at the center of the world's retail model.

- Millions of people get their first job at McDonald's. It may be just a temporary thing while they are in school or a part-time job as a teenager. But whether they are aware of it or not, their McDonald's experience provides incredible business education for those who are keen observers of what is happening around them.
- There are more than thirty-one thousand McDonald's stores in the world, most of which are owned and operated by franchisees. Throughout the corporation's history this model has provided hundreds of thousands of people the opportunity to own and operate their own business. Few companies in the world give more entrepreneurs this opportunity than McDonald's.
- McDonald's employs 1.5 million people around the world, which in and of itself is an enormous contribution to society.
- McDonald's stores are located in 119 countries.
- No two countries that have McDonald's stores have ever gone to war against each other.
- McDonald's feeds 47 million customers every day.
- The training and development available to those who commit themselves to a career at McDonald's are world class.
- McDonald's is committed to giving back to the local communities that have made them successful. The most obvious expression of this is the Ronald McDonald House charities, which provide somewhere for the parents and siblings of sick children to stay while their loved ones are in the hospital.

- McDonald's has produced more millionaires than Warren Buffett.

You may not like the food, but it is indisputable that for more than fifty years McDonald's has been making incredible contributions to the lives of millions of employees, shareholders, entrepreneurs, and communities. McDonald's has made the fulfillment of millions of ordinary people's dreams possible—including many of my own.

An entry level job with McDonald's has been the beginning of great things for hundreds of thousands of people. Charlie Bell took a job with McDonald's when he was fifteen, in suburban Sydney, Australia. At forty-four he was named CEO of McDonald's worldwide. Other McDonald's employees have gone on to dominate every field imaginable. A short list includes: musician extraordinaire Seal; actresses Sharon Stone and Rachel McAdams; Olympic gold medalist Carl Lewis; comedian and legendary host of *The Tonight Show* Jay Leno; NASCAR sensation Tony Stewart; country music star Shania Twain; former White House chief of staff Andy Card; and Jeff Bezos, the founder and CEO of Amazon.com.

So it is important to affirm that McDonald's is not just about cooking burgers. McDonald's has helped millions of its employees to attain college degrees, pursue their dreams, and turn what they learned working for McDonald's into rewarding careers in marketing, real estate, training and development, design, business management, and as entrepreneurs.

One of the dreams McDonald's is helping me achieve is my own financial freedom. And in the process, another dream has emerged. For more than a decade now I have watched thousands of people work in dozens of roles at McDonald's. Society tells them that this is a dead end job. Most of them have never even thought about being financially free, and if they did stumble upon the idea, they would immediately assume that it was an impossible goal. Witnessing this ignited within me a dream to help these people, and anyone else who is interested, to work toward and claim financial freedom.

I first decided to become financially free when I was seventeen. It wasn't a "that would be nice" thought—it was a serious decision, although at the time I had no idea how I would achieve it. I'm not sure why I decided to be financially free. Perhaps it was my father exposing me to the nicer parts of the city and the finer things in life, even though we could not afford many of them. Or maybe it was the tension that seemed to surround money in so many relationships. Regardless, I decided that I wanted financial freedom in my future and have pursued it ever since.

I would like to invite you to make that decision now. Even if you think it is impossible for you, even if you don't know how you are going to do it, and even if you have no money today. Decide now that you are going to be financially free someday in the future.

The genius of McDonald's is the systems that drive the business.

There are systems for everything at McDonald's. There is a system for cooking and preparing burgers, but way beyond that there is a system for every operation that has to take place with any regularity. One of the most ingenious examples is the ordering system. As a twenty-something I was able to do a simple stock check, answer certain computer-generated questions, and as a result hundreds of food and paper products would be ordered. In the same way I was able to schedule hundreds of crew members for their shifts each week. McDonald's is a culture of systems.

The reason the systems are so important is because systems drive behavior—and success. Find the best way and then build a system to ensure that it gets done that way every time.

The beauty of the systems is that anyone willing to make an effort can succeed. The systems are not complex; in fact, their genius is found in their simplicity. The systems have been tried and tested, and are continually refined, to deliver the very best results. Stick to the systems and you will succeed. Stray from the systems and you will almost certainly fail.

In this book I will present to you a system designed to help you achieve financial freedom. Anyone willing to make an effort can follow the system. The system is not complex; in fact, in a world of ever-increasing complexity it contains a rare simplicity. Stick to the system and you will experience financial success beyond your wildest imaginings.

CHAPTER TWO

A BILLION-DOLLAR
FAMILY NAME

Money and the creation of wealth are not that difficult to understand. You save some money, invest it, and it multiplies. Save a little bit, often enough, for long enough, and it will become an enormous fortune. The problem is that most people cannot think beyond today and what they want to spend their money on right now. They do not have a vision for their life ten years from now, or twenty years from now, and nobody saves money for a future that they have not yet imagined.

Even more so, most people do not think about the next generation of their family. When faced with a decision, the American Indians asked themselves, "How will this decision affect the seventh generation of our people?" This ability to get beyond ourselves and to consider time horizons is an incredible skill that can be nurtured and will serve us well at work, in relationships, and in our quest for financial freedom.

Few families build a billion-dollar family name in one generation. Which means that somebody, generations before the family became billionaires, had a vision for their family to become super-wealthy. Now, you may not think it is possible for your family to become one of those billion-dollar families. I will be honest with you: In your lifetime it is not likely. But if you are willing to think beyond your lifetime and beyond your children's lifetime, and follow the system I lay out for you in this book, you will live an incredible life, so will your children, and your grandchildren just might inherit a billion-dollar family name.

Let me show you how.

Accumulating Incredible Wealth Is Not That Difficult

Allow me to explain it another way. Think about the wealthiest family you know. Have you ever wondered how they became so wealthy? You may think they became wealthy because they own some car dealerships or a restaurant, but nobody gets wealthy by merely possessing a good business. They may make a lot of money this way, but being wealthy does not simply come from earning a lot of money. Becoming wealthy comes from saving and investing.

Now consider the wealthiest families in the world. People read about these families and salivate over their wealth and lifestyles. The wealthiest family in the world is the Walton family. Together they have $83.2 billion. How did they get it? They inherited it. How did their parents and grandparents amass such an incredible fortune? Most would say by founding Wal-Mart, but they would be wrong. The Walton family has an incredible fortune today because someone in their family tree saved and invested some of what they earned.

It is also important to note that most people consider this kind of wealth to be for other people and other families. Most people would never consider it possible for their family to possess that kind of wealth. But they are wrong. If you want your family to be one of the richest families in the world, simply follow the plan I will lay out in this book.

I can hear the doubts in your mind, so let's cut to the chase.

If you invest $1 for forty years at 10 percent it will be worth $45 forty years from now.

In the following chapters I am going to share with you three savings plans. If you begin the first at eighteen years of age, as I did, you will have $32,369 by the time you are twenty-five. If you invest that money as I suggest and receive an average annual return of 10 percent, forty years later, when you are sixty-five, it will have grown to $1,456,609—even if you didn't add another penny to it since you were twenty-five.

If instead you follow the second savings plan I lay out, you will have $61,357 by the time you are twenty-five. If you invest that and receive a return of 10 percent, forty years later, at sixty-five you, will have almost $3 million.

If instead you follow the third savings plan, you will have $135,326 by the time you are twenty-five. If you invest this in the same way described above, by the time you are sixty-five it will have grown to $6 million.

Now, that would not make your family one of the wealthiest in the world, but suppose you kept saving throughout your working life, and then consider your 401k plan. You might never have to touch your nest egg, and you could leave it to the next generation—your children.

If they didn't touch it for forty years, it would then be $274 million. If your children worked to make their own way in life and left it to your grandchildren, and they kept it invested for forty years, it would be more than $10 billion.

If your grandchildren had the discipline and desire to grow this fortune and invested it for another forty years, your great-grandchildren would inherit $450 billion. Two more generations and your heirs would be the stewards of $24 trillion—more than any family in the world today. All this in just five generations, because you saved and invested about $135,000.

That is usually how dynastic wealth is built—the sacrifice of one man or woman, and mutigenerational discipline.

The Average Person

Now let us consider the average person. The average American has a net worth at sixty-five of $232,000. Across all age groups the median net worth of an American family is $120,300. And if the big picture is a surprise to many, the little picture is downright frightening. More than 43 percent of American families spend more than they earn every year; the average American household carries more than $8,000 worth of credit card debt, and personal bankruptcies have doubled in the past decade.

And still, we teach our children nothing about personal finance in school.

I was fortunate that my father and brothers taught me a great deal about money. More than that, they gave me a desire to know more and more about the dynamics of personal finance. Most people are not this fortunate. It does not make their parents bad people, because nobody ever talked to them about the unchanging laws of money either. We don't teach it in high school, we don't teach it in college, and we don't teach it in the business world. Yet few things affect our lives more than our ability to manage our personal finances.

In the corporate world I am amazed at how often we put people in charge of million-dollar budgets who cannot manage their own personal budget.

I am not naïve enough to think I can change the whole system, but this book is my own small contribution to turning the tide on what I think is one of the great tragedies of modern society.

The average American has little more at retirement than a slave to show for a lifetime of work. Our first reaction may be to say that people are not paid enough or that it is because the rich take advantage of the working class. But the truth is, the great majority of people make enough to save a little, and if you save a little for a long time, you end up with an awful lot.

The average American at retirement has little to show for a lifetime of work because he or she either:

(a) was never taught the unchanging laws of money,

(b) ignored the unchanging laws of money,

(c) lacked the desire and/or discipline to save and invest, or

(d) experienced some combination of the above.

By the time you are finished reading this book I want you to be convinced of two things:

1. The average person is capable of amassing wealth beyond his or her imagination simply by working hard, saving diligently, and investing wisely; and more importantly,

2. that you are capable of amassing a fortune to both enjoy in your lifetime and pass on to future generations.

If I do not convince you of this last point, I will have failed.

There Is More to Life Than Money

When you tell people that you are writing a book, they automatically ask what it is about. When you tell them you are writing a book about financial freedom, I cannot tell you how many people say, "There is more to life than money."

They are right, but there is more to life with money. Mae West, the American actress, playwright, and screenwriter said, "I've been rich and I've been poor. Believe me, rich is better," and I think most people would agree with her.

Money is not everything. This book is not about the

idolization of money and those who possess it. I think of this book as a much more practical guide to the accumulation of the kind of wealth that can give you and your family opportunities.

So, yes, it is the things that money cannot buy that are most important—health, love, trust, faith, friendship, family, wisdom, and finding what you love and doing it. But too often a lack of money destroys our chance at these things. This book is not about making money more important than these things; it is about understanding how money can support the people and things that matter most in your life.

What Is Financial Freedom?

I have noticed we hear about financial freedom less and less. The reason, I believe, is because most people think it is impossible to be financially free. But you are quickly discovering, I hope, that this is not the case. Interestingly, the entry for "financial freedom" (or, to be precise, "financial independence") in the world's largest encyclopedia—Wikipedia—is a short one, unlike the many far more extensive entries found on the site. Financial freedom is possible, and we should be talking about it more than we are. We should be learning about it and teaching our children about it at home and in school.

So what is financial freedom? Well, the answer to this question is different for everyone. Some people think financial freedom is being able to buy whatever you need. Others think it means being able to buy whatever you want. There are also those who think financial freedom is being completely debt free. Still others think earning a salary that allows them to live comfortably is financial freedom.

If you ask one hundred people to define "financial freedom," you are likely to get a hundred different answers. The reason is because "freedom" is a deeply personal thing. Even locked up in a jail cell, I suspect Nelson Mandela and Mahatma Gandhi felt freer than many people ever do.

We often can gain a great deal of insight into something by studying its opposite. In this case consider financial slavery, or just slavery itself. The difference between a free man and a slave is that the free man can do as he wishes and the slave must do as his master tells him to.

We abolished the ownership of slaves, but I am not sure we have abolished slavery. There are many people today who live in conditions as inhumane as the conditions many slaves were afforded by their masters in centuries past. The slavery of our modern world is financial slavery.

So who are the financially free? Those who can do as they wish.

I like working. I'm not in a hurry to retire. I enjoy my work. If I won $10 million today, I would still go to work tomorrow. But it is one thing to work because you want to and another thing altogether to work because you have to.

Most people work because they have to. If today they won enough money to take care of themselves for the rest of their life, today would be their last day at work. Now, perhaps they would go back to school or pursue another career if they had all the money in the world—but they don't, because they are enslaved financially, in large ways or small. Their master is the bank that holds their mortgage, or the credit card company, or their unrestrained desire for consumption.

You can decide what it means for you to be financially free, or how much money that would require, but the most universally accepted definition of financial freedom is "having enough money to do what you want to do when you want to do it." For some that may mean sitting on the porch of their $95,000 home in Iowa reading books all day long. For another that might mean getting around the world in their $50 million Gulfstream 550 private jet. These are personal preferences, but the premise remains the same: If they had more money, most people would live their lives differently. You have got to decide if the way you would live your life differently is worth striving for.

What Would You Do If You Had Flipping Millions?

So let me ask you, if you had $1 million in the bank, how would you live your life differently?

Take a moment. Think about it. Really consider the possibilities. And write down three things that you would do if you had $1 million.

1. _____

2. _____

3. _____

Now let's take it a step further. How would you live your life differently if you had $10 million?

That's a lot of money, so think about it. Ten million dollars invested in triple tax-free municipal bonds would net you a tax-free income of approximately $500,000 a year forever.

Write down three things you would do if you had $10 million.

1. _____

2. _____

3. _____

Now one more step. How would you live your life differently if you had $100 million?

It's just another zero, but it ushers in another universe of possibilities. Private jets, luxury homes around the world, a personal chef, a Black American Express card, and the ability to do an awful lot of good are all within reach now.

Write down three things you would do if you had $100 million.

1. _____

2. _____

3. _____

Again, you may be tempted to think that you will never have $100 million. Be that as it may, following the advice in this book, you can set your family up to have much more than $100 million in future generations. So it is important that you begin to formulate a vision for that money. When thinking about $1 million or $10 million, most people think about how that money could improve their lives and the lives of their immediate families. But when it comes to $100 million, most people move beyond themselves and start to consider how they can make a difference in the world.

There are many ways you can influence what future generations of your family do with the wealth that you are creating for them to enjoy and share. For this reason it is critical that you begin to think about what could be possible with the vast sum of money you are going to be making available to them.

(Visit *www.moneyclassroom.com* to see how other people answered these questions . . . and others.)

If you have taken this exercise seriously, you have now envisioned what you would do with wealth if you were able to acquire it. Does what you have envisioned excite you? Is it worth working toward? What are you willing to sacrifice in order to achieve it?

Most people never take the time to envision how life would be different if they saved, invested, and began to build some real wealth. Without that vision, it is impossible to make the sacrifices necessary to turn our hopes and dreams into reality.

Get clear about what your financial hopes and dreams are. Create plans and goals that will take you one step closer each day to achieving and experiencing them. Get clear about what you want the money for. If you don't know what you want the money for—you won't make the sacrifices to earn, save, invest, and multiply it.

Difficult and Rare

People who do not believe that financial freedom is impossible still tend to believe that it is too difficult. Of course it is difficult. It is difficult to start on your way to it, and it is difficult to continue there. It is difficult to earn your first thousand dollars, and it is even more difficult to save your first thousand dollars. It is difficult to maintain the discipline of saving and investing. And once you have amassed a fortune (great or small), it is difficult to put it to work so that it reproduces at a rate worthy of the discipline you have displayed in order to save it. It is difficult to make the right decisions about how and where and with whom to invest your money.

And, no doubt, it is tricky. If it were easy, it would be common. Everyone wants the difficult things, but few are willing to pay the price to accomplish them. That's why it's rare when someone actually does.

The quest for financial freedom will test you, but that does not mean you should get discouraged and turn back. It simply means you should prepare and equip yourself for a challenging journey. And no matter how tough the journey may seem to be, it is worth it, and you need to keep reminding yourself of that.

I'd like to think that the people around you would encourage and support you in this journey, but the truth is, most people won't understand what you are doing or why you are doing it. If they understood it, they would be doing it themselves. But they have been seduced by a culture of instant gratification and obsession with appearances.

The slightest pressure consistently applied over a long period of time can create or destroy most things. If you place a slab of rock under a dripping faucet for a day, the rock will become damp. If you leave the faucet dripping for a year, the water will create a slight indentation in the rock. If you leave the faucet dripping for a hundred years, the water will create a hole in the rock slab. That's all it takes to build wealth—time and pressure. A little bit of pressure—saving and investing—consistently applied over time can create an incredible fortune.

For example, if a person saved $1 a day for her entire life and invested it with a return of 10 percent, she would retire at sixty-five years of age with $2,404,853. One dollar a day is just like that dripping faucet.

It is difficult, but it is not impossible.

What makes it difficult is not that it requires some extraordinary set of skills, but that it requires the discipline of consistency in a world dominated by erratic impulse.

The Unchanging Laws of Money

If you Google the term "personal finance," you will discover there are more than 100 million search results. If you search "personal finance" on Amazon.com you will discover more than thirty-eight thousand books in print on this single subject. And yet the laws of money are unchanging. Every one of these books, websites, and articles speaks to one of the seven unchanging laws of money. Most of them overcomplicate the unchanging laws.

These are the seven unchanging laws of money. Learn them. Apply them to the way you live each day. Ignore them at your financial peril.

1. Save . . . and begin saving early.
2. Control your expenses.
3. Make your money multiply. . . . Invest.
4. Guard your money against loss.
5. Make your home an investment.
6. Ensure a future income for yourself and your family . . . by developing a career, improving yourself, and investing.
7. Work and study to increase your ability to earn.

The laws of money have never changed. People add nuances here and there to make them appear new and fresh, but the truth is they are time-tested and stable. Many people dismiss them because the rules seem old-fashioned and we live in a culture obsessed with all things new and modern. But these seven laws are like an old treasure map. You wouldn't throw a treasure map away just because it was old. The value of a treasure map does not come from its age. The value of a treasure map is determined by whether or not it leads to treasure.

These seven unchanging laws of money are an old treasure map, but they still lead to treasure.

It's pretty simple when you have it explained to you, though I would not want you to confuse simple with easy. "Save, invest, and live beneath your means" doesn't sound like a master plan, but it is a sure way to financial freedom. Save, invest, and live beneath your means. I know, it doesn't sound sexy and cool, but let me assure you that having $5 million when you retire is.

The Four Stages of Your Financial Life

In this book we are going to explore the four stages of your financial life and what you can expect in each of them if you follow my plan. The four stages are:

Stage One—Right Now
Stage Two—Quality of Life
Stage Three—Retirement
Stage Four—Legacy

The first stage deals with the next eight years, beginning today. The second stage deals with the years between nine years from today and when you retire. The third stage deals with the years from the day you retire until the day you die. And the fourth stage deals with the financial legacy you will leave behind when you leave this earth.

In each stage I will outline specific goals and objectives, but it will be up to you to put dollar amounts to each of those goals and objectives according to your income, desire to build wealth, and other commitments.

In many cases, I will offer three options—good, better, and best. If you have not done so already, you will quickly discover that there can be an enormous difference between good, better, and best. For example, the difference between saving $32,000 and $135,000 in Stage One may seem like $103,000, but in fact by retirement that difference is the gap between $1,400,000 and $6,000,000, assuming a ten percent return rate. So a $103,000 difference at age twenty-five equates to a difference of more than three-and-a-half million dollars at age sixty-five.

Thomas Jefferson, the third president of the United States, observed, "We rarely repent of having eaten too little." In the same way, you will never regret having saved too much.

So push yourself a little. I have never met anyone who was sorry to have saved his or her money. We seldom repent of having spent too little. But I have met many people burdened by debt who regret having spent too much.

CHAPTER THREE

FIRST THINGS FIRST

Where do we start? A solid and consistent savings and investing plan is the road to financial freedom. But you cannot save if you do not earn. So the first step is to create a source of income, and for most people that means getting a job. You have to earn money before you can save money.

What job should you get? Any job, to start. Eventually we all want to be doing something we feel passionate about, but in the beginning we don't really know what that is. The world is full of stories about people who wanted a certain job their whole life, but when they got it discovered they didn't like it at all.

You discover what you love doing by doing things you don't love doing. You discover what you are good at by trying things and working out what you are not good at.

Whether you are just out of high school, or just out of college, or about to be in either of these scenarios, my counsel to you would be: Don't get too picky—get started. Explore the opportunities, weigh your options, but then act. Take a job. Don't sit around waiting for the perfect job.

Eventually you will work your way into something you really love doing. But it takes time and a certain self-awareness that only comes from doing different things. Those different things can be part of the same job, or parts of different jobs within the same company. But we work our way into the perfect job for us by doing, not by thinking or planning.

I love working for McDonald's. I consider myself fortunate that the first company I came to work for provided me the opportunities to grow and learn, and that it was a company that invests in its people. Not everyone loves working at McDonald's, but I always have. From the day I started working here I have studied people and systems, and been enamored with the story of Ray Kroc and his dreams.

Are there good days and bad days? Yes. But I think that is true of every job, even fantasy jobs like playing professional sports.

Be a Great Employee

Once you have a job, whatever job that may be—give it your best. Be a great employee. It may sound trite, but very few people wake up in the morning and consciously think about being a great employee. In fact, most people never think about it. The result, of course, is that they are only looking out for what they can get, and many are committed to doing as little as possible.

This is theft. When we act this way, we are stealing from our employers, we are stealing from society, and we are stealing from ourselves. When we don't give our best at what we do, we rob ourselves of the opportunity to grow and learn, and that in turn limits our future.

If you are going to take a job, decide to be a great employee. This is how you do it. . . .

1. WORK HARD

Nothing will take the place of hard work. It is good for your career, and it is good for you as a person. Hard work builds character, and regardless of whether your hard work is recognized or rewarded, working hard is deeply satisfying. Going to work and not throwing yourself into your work kills the soul. Besides the intrinsic value of hard work, that you are capable of this sort of discipline is something you need to know. Knowing this makes you approach life and work differently, even at the times when you don't have to push yourself to full capacity.

Those who are willing to work hard will always have a job and will always get ahead. It seems that fewer and fewer people are actually willing to work hard. Too many want to loaf their way through the workweek. So those of us who are willing to get in and work hard will be more richly rewarded with every passing year, regardless of the field we work in.

Nobody has said it better than coach John Wooden: "Why is it so hard for so many to realize that winners are usually the ones who work harder, work longer, and as a result, perform better?"

2. DON'T BE LIKE EVERYONE ELSE

It is human nature to relax, take it easy, and only do what you absolutely have to do. Most employees only work at about 60 percent capacity. This type of mediocrity is very self-destructive, and truth be told, it takes more energy to sustain mediocrity than it does to grow in excellence. You have to really try to stay ordinary.

When you go to work, don't let the people around you determine how you work. Remember, they probably go to work just to survive, while you have a dream of financial freedom you are working toward.

In your manager's eyes, how you do one thing is how you do everything. There is no point appealing for a better job with more pay and more responsibility if you don't do your current job well.

If you want to rise through the ranks of a company, which will increase your chances of financial freedom, you need to differentiate yourself from other employees.

Here are a few pointers: Show up to work a little early. On time is just expected, but you want to stand out. Push yourself and work hard. Most employees have to be pushed hard by their managers. Be a self-starter. Take initiative. If you see a simple task that needs to be done, do it. Don't worry about getting noticed or getting the credit. Much of what you do will not get noticed, some of what you do you will not get credit for, but doing it changes who you are as a person—and it will be impossible to ignore the type of person you are. Be a standout performer. Even if everyone else is just getting by with 60 or 70 percent effort, give your best. Don't waste time.

Don't wait to be asked to do something. If you don't have something to do, find something to do. Keep yourself busy—it is good for you, good for your career, and good for the business. Don't be one of those people who constantly wish they were somewhere else; make the most of where you are. Don't be ordinary, even in ordinary things. Do the ordinary things extraordinarily well.

There is no easier way to stand out from the crowd than by being attentive to the details of your work. We live in a world where very few people take care of the details and most people despise them. Take care of the details and you will stand out as being very different in today's workforce.

Every moment is an opportunity to invest in yourself. Which one, hard work or the bare minimum, will help you become financially free? The answer, of course, is hard work. Which one, standing around doing nothing or proactively looking for something to do, will help you become financially free? Proactively looking for something to do. Use each moment to grow and learn, but also to demonstrate that there is a difference between you and other employees.

In essence, much of what I have described here is the essence of a leader. The earlier you start behaving like one, the more likely it is that you will become one.

3. ADD VALUE

Most people are constantly consumed by the question "What's in it for me?" When it comes to work, there is plenty in it for you: salary or wages; training and development; experience and new skills that make you more valuable in the future as an employee; an increasing chance of better opportunities for you and your family in the future; a greater probability with each passing day of becoming financially free; and any number of other benefits.

There's plenty in it for you, so let that question take a place in the back of your mind and move on to a question that will make you rich in every sense of the word: "What contribution can I make that will add value to this team, project, or business?"

Business is about adding value. If a business does not add value to its customers' lives, it will go out of business. If an employee does not add value to a business, that employee will eventually find him- or herself without a job. But more important, the more value a business adds to its customers' lives, the more customers will reward that business with sales, profits, and word-of-mouth marketing.

Think of yourself as a business. Your employer is your best customer—and your only customer. The more value you add to your customer's life (in this case the business you work for), the more your customer will reward you. In this case the rewards come in the form of promotions, pay increases, bonuses, and more opportunities for training and development, which increase your chances of advancement.

If you want to be a great employee, add value.

4. MAKE IT HAPPEN

In my career I have been sent on some kamikaze assignments. A couple of years ago I was sent to manage a store that was losing $100,000 a year. I am sure that there were people who were hoping I would fail. But within a year, that store was making $200,000.

Great employees develop a reputation for making it happen. It's amazing how many people sit around and say that certain problems cannot be solved, or that it is not their problem. You make more money if it is your job to solve problems. Leaders and managers make more money than front-line employees because it is their job to solve the problems.

So wherever you are on the corporate ladder, start solving problems. The more you demonstrate your willingness to get in and try to solve problems, the more likely you are to be promoted to a position that requires your problem-solving skills. In the meantime, you are learning how to solve problems just by jumping in and trying—and all the time your future earning potential is increasing.

Get a reputation for being a team member who can make it happen. Solve problems, exude a can-do attitude, and step it up a notch when the important tasks come along.

Being a great employee isn't that hard, it's just that so few people ever think on this level.

5. MAKE YOUR BOSS LOOK GOOD

If you are going to rise up in any organization, you need advocates. An advocate is someone who vouches for you. Your most likely advocate is your manager.

When there is a promotion to be had, your manager's boss is going to come to him and ask him who he thinks would be best for the job. Your name has to be the first name that comes to your manager's mind.

You need to get key people on your side. This doesn't mean you have to kiss up. The ones who have to kiss up are those who don't work hard, stand out from the crowd, add value, and make it happen. A manager is not going to recommend these people for promotion anyway, because if they do a bad job they will make her look bad because she suggested them.

Each day ask yourself, "How can I make my boss's job easier today?" Too many employees only make more work for their managers. Your job is to keep whatever you can off your manager's plate, while at the same time recognizing when something belongs there.

6. KEEP LEARNING

Those who achieve excellence in any field are continuous learners. Michael Jordan never stopped learning about basketball, and Tiger Woods can never learn too much about golf. Ray Kroc never tired of learning about the burger business, and Bill Gates is still as hungry to learn about the next wave of technology as he was forty years ago.

Benjamin Barber wrote,

I divide the world into learners and non-learners. There are people who learn, who are open to what happens around them, who listen, who hear the lessons. When they do something stupid, they don't do it again. And when they do something that works a little bit, they do it even better and harder next time. The question to ask is not whether you are a success or a failure, but whether you are a learner or a non-learner.

Great employees approach every day as an opportunity to learn, whether it is a workday or not. Every day, make it a goal to learn something new about yourself, your job, your company, or your industry. Just one thing. It is amazing how quickly this knowledge begins to build, and how significantly this habit can change the trajectory of your career.

7. OBSERVE PEOPLE

One of the ways we can learn every day is by observing people. This is one of the most powerful habits you can acquire. Observe your customers so that you can anticipate their needs. Observe your teammates so that you can imitate what they are good at, and eradicate from your own behavior anything you see them doing that is not productive and conducive to your team's goals. Observe your manager to anticipate his or her needs.

But also, observe the different managers you have throughout the course of your career. Every time your manager says or does something that energizes you, make a note of it. Anytime your manager does something that deflates or disengages you, make a note of that too.

One day you are going to be a manager yourself. When that day comes, you will have two lists: one with the effective and the other with the ineffective ways you have been managed throughout your career. Being a good manager is about doing and saying all the good things that your managers once did and said to you, and not doing and saying all the things that managers once did and said that deflated and disengaged you.

In the past fifty years we have witnessed tremendous technological advancement in all areas of business and life. And yet on both sides of every business transaction we still find human beings. Get to know people. Observe them. Learn to anticipate their needs and next moves. This fundamental understanding of people will become one of your key competitive advantages as your career progresses.

The Meaning of Work

Too many people think work is just about making money, and it may seem strange in a book about becoming financially free that I would discourage such a view, but anyone who thinks that the primary value and meaning of work is making money will never be happy at work.

You may also be tempted to say that working for McDonald's is not very meaningful. This is a common mistake. On the one hand, McDonald's is about burgers and fries, but to separate the Happy Meals from the opportunities this company has made available to tens of millions of entrepreneurs and employees over its history would be a mistake.

Your work allows you to earn a living, provides financial and material sustenance for you and your family, and fuels your chances of financial freedom, but these are all secondary. There are much more significant aspects to our work, among them our personal development and contribution to society.

The personal development aspect of work is more significant to our quest for financial freedom than the wages or salary we receive. The reason is because the more we develop both inside and outside the workplace, the more our capacity to earn in the future increases.

Increasing capacity to earn in the future is the ultimate compounding investment.

Beyond providing for our material needs and giving us opportunities for personal development, all honest work also contains an aspect of contributing to society. My work feeds people, provides employment for others, and distributes profits to shareholders and charitable organizations.

Work has meaning way beyond the paycheck, and the more you are able to recognize that, the more likely it is that the size of your paycheck will increase.

CHAPTER FOUR

GETTING STARTED—
FINANCIAL BASICS

Most people never arrive at a day when they don't have to worry about money. Sure, there are plenty of people who don't worry about money, but that is the result of a strong dose of denial and avoidance; those people should worry about money. It is a tragedy that millions of people, indeed the great majority of people, after working for a lifetime still have to worry about money.

Someday, wouldn't you like to *not* have to worry about money anymore? I am going to assume the answer to that question is yes, and continue to lay before you a plan to arrive at that day sooner rather than later.

You are already a lot closer to that day since you picked up this book. With every page you turn, I hope this book is arousing desire and delivering life-changing knowledge—the desire and knowledge to become financially free.

Every journey toward financial freedom begins in exactly

the same way. Behind even the most incredible wealth you will find a person who learned and applied the basics of wealth creation. You may have to go back several generations in some families to find the person with whom it all began. But they are always there . . . and they are always connoisseurs of the basics.

The key-to financial success is not get-rich-quick schemes or complex financial instruments. Football teams win championships by mastering the basics. Ordinary people become wealthy by mastering the basics.

This chapter is about the basics of wealth creation. Here you will find the ideas and techniques you will need in order to master the four stages of your financial life. In the process, you will learn how to develop the disciplines that will allow you to prosper financially for the rest of your life.

When NASA sends a shuttle into space, it uses 97 percent of its fuel at takeoff. It is hard to get the shuttle off the ground, but once it is moving it requires almost no fuel. When you first begin your quest for financial freedom, you are going to need a lot of effort to get started, but once you are in the flow of your plan, it will become virtually effortless.

The Gratification Question

The answer to this one question will determine whether or not you will ever be financially free. Are you willing to delay gratification?

If you are not willing to delay gratification, you will never be financially free. Personal finance is one of those arenas where you cannot have your cake and eat it too. The inability to delay gratification is the mark of almost every failure in our lives. And the incredible successes of all heroes, leaders, legends, and champions are marked by a greater than average ability to delay gratification.

Your ability to succeed at anything is dependent on your ability to delay gratification.

The problem is we live in a world where instant gratification isn't fast enough anymore. People seem more and more impatient with each passing year. Whether they are driving to work or standing in line for their Quarter Pounder, people seem to have a diminishing ability to wait. And waiting is a huge part of any successful saving and investing plan. Work hard, save hard, invest wisely, and wait. And the waiting can seem endless at times, when compared with the rush of instant gratification that comes from buying whatever it is that has captured your attention this week.

Developing an approach to money will not only lead to financial success, but will also help you to acquire skills that can be applied to every area of life, including relationships and marriage, raising children, your career and business, and health and wellness.

The bottom line is this: If you can acquire the ability to delay gratification in your life, one day you will be financially free, and you will probably amass wealth beyond your imagination. If you cannot acquire the ability to delay gratification, regardless of how much money you earn and at what rate your earnings increase, you are never likely to be financially free. It is the indispensible discipline.

Will it be easy? Absolutely not. By now you are probably figuring out that this is far from a get-rich-quick book. This book is filled with honest truths about how people who are never likely to earn a million dollars a year, or even hundreds of thousands of dollars a year, can accomplish financial freedom.

So, if it is not going to be easy, it is important to get really clear about why you want it. Why do you want to be financially free?

Get Clear About Your Financial Goals

If your "why" is not compelling enough, you won't build a plan and stick to the plan. So take some time to think specifically about all the anguish and misery you and those you love will experience if you don't strive for a place of financial freedom. Then, get really clear about the incredible opportunities you and your loved ones will experience if you do begin and make this journey with me. Desire. Goals. Plan. Action.

There are many practical lessons I can share with you to help you to create financial freedom, but unless you get clear about what that means to you and why you want it, you won't get there. You have to get in touch with the desire to be financially free. You have to get in touch with how your life will be different if you walk the path I am describing in this book. Our lives are ruled by desire. Some people are able to direct their desires, and others are ruled by their desires. Your desire for financial freedom has to be stronger than the many desires you have to spend money on any number of unnecessary things every day.

This desire may not be strong enough yet, but don't get discouraged. We are not born with the desire for financial freedom. The desire can be sought, nurtured, and attained. How? Well, if I am doing my job as an author of a book about financial freedom, as you are reading this book your desire for financial freedom should be growing. The desire also grows as you see your savings grow. Spending time with other people who have the same desire for financial freedom fans the flame of that desire. And reading books about people who have built incredible fortunes increases the desire also.

The first step is desire. The second step is to have real and specific goals. Your financial goals can take many forms. Here are some examples:

- I want to pay off all my credit card debt in the next year.
- I want to save $X from every paycheck.
- I want to save $X each year for the next ten years.
- I want to save X percent of every dollar I ever earn.
- I want to have $X invested by the time I retire.
- I want to have saved and invested $X by the time I am age Y.
- I want my investments to be producing a non-exertive income of $X by the time I am age Y.
- I want to be financially free by age Y.

Henry David Thoreau observed, "In the long run, men only hit what they aim at." Your financial goals give you something to aim at. They are practical expressions of your financial dreams and desires.

So what will it take for you to be financially free? Most people I talk to don't know the answer to this question. Those who do have an answer usually pluck it out of the sky. They don't base their answer on any study of their financial needs. Let's take a look at the question.

If you didn't get to work next month, how much money would you need to cover your regular and necessary expenses?

For example: Susan is twenty-four years old and lives in Iowa. These are her monthly expenses:

Rent	$350
Car Payment	$250
Insurance	$120
Food	$180
Utilities	$115
Other/Misc.	$85
Total	$1,100

To maintain this lifestyle, which does not include shopping for clothes or entertainment, Susan would need $1,100 a month or $13,200 each year. If we assume she has an invested lump sum that produces a return of 5 percent after tax, Susan would need that sum to be $264,000 to have a basic level of financial freedom.

If you complete the above list and your total comes to

$2,500 a month, then you would require $600,000. If your total is $5,000 a month, you would need $1,200,000. This is of course a lot of money, but the first level of financial freedom usually does not require as much money as people think. In fact, the problem is, most people have never really stopped to think about it.

Now calculate what you would need to be financially free. Put together your list of essential monthly expenses, then multiply it by 12 (to give an annual number), then multiply that by 20 (to give the lump sum you would need to invest at a 5 percent after-tax return).

Most people don't need anywhere near as much as they think they do for basic financial freedom. But most people have never taken the time to really work out how much basic financial freedom would require.

Your financial goals will likely change over time. If you follow the system I am laying out in this book, ten or twenty years from now you will very likely look at the financial goals you wrote down today and wonder why they were so small. So take a few minutes now and write down your financial goals. Where do you want to be financially by the end of this year? In five years? In ten years? In twenty years?

What's a Dollar Worth?

We have all heard people say, "It's just a dollar!" or five dollars, or twenty dollars. But it is never just a dollar, as we will soon discover. Money wants to procreate, and it is not particular about who it procreates with. You can spend it, but then it will procreate with someone else. Too many people overlook or underestimate money's ability to multiply.

Imagine you and I meet for a game of golf. On the first tee, I say to you, "Shall we have a bet?" You say, "Sure, what did you have in mind?"

I suggest that we play for $1 on the first hole and double our bet every hole. It's only a dollar. It seems harmless, so you agree.

The second hole we play for $2. The third we play for $4. By the ninth hole, we are playing for $256. On fifteen we are playing for $16,388, so I hope you brought your game with you. By the eighteenth hole, we are playing for $131,072. By now you may have learned a very expensive lesson in the power of money and multiplication.

Consider it in another way. You see an advertisement for a television with a price tag of $3,000. How much does that TV cost? Most would say $3,000. They would be wrong.

On average in the United States, we pay 7 percent sales tax, so the TV is now $3,210.

The IRS does not allow you to buy your state-of-the-art TV with pre-tax dollars, so in order for you to buy that TV (assuming you pay 25 percent taxes), you must earn $4,280.

If you are twenty-five years old when you are considering this television purchase, and assuming that you are able to invest your money in such a way that it doubles every ten years—a conservative estimate—when you're thirty-five years old, that $4,280, if invested rather than spent on a TV, will have grown to $8,560. At forty-five, it will have grown to

$17,120. And by retirement at the age of sixty-five, it will have grown to $68,480.

Do you really need that $68,480 television? I am not saying don't have a television. I am simply encouraging you to be aware of what things really cost. If instead you bought a TV for $1,500, you would have an extra $34,240 at retirement.

Of course, the real cost of things for most people is time. If you need $30,000 a year to live on, the cost of that TV is really two years of your life.

Think before you spend.

Understand Your Money Patterns

It is said that every journey toward something is a journey away from something, and sometimes it seems just as important to know what you are journeying away from as it is to know what you are journeying toward. In your journey toward financial freedom, it is critical that you work out what habits will help you achieve your financial goals, but it is also important that you identify what habits are stopping you from achieving your financial goals.

One of the first steps in becoming financially free is working out why you are not already well on the way. It may be that you are a teenager and have not even had your first job yet. If that is the case, you are way ahead of the game. But for most of us it is probably because we have some habits that are causing our personal finances to self-destruct on a monthly basis.

One of Socrates' guiding rules was "Know thyself." There

is no arena in our lives where the application of this wisdom will not lead to increasing success and fulfillment. This is particularly true in the area of personal finances.

For the great majority of people there comes a time in each month when they have more month left than they do money. Very often, if you ask them what they spent all their money on, they will just look at you with a blank stare. Too many people honestly don't know what they spent their money on.

We have explored how saving small amounts of money can add up to enormous fortunes over time, and what is true on the positive side (saving) and also true on the negative side (spending). We can spend a lot of money, a little bit at a time, on a lot of nothing.

By now the Latte Factor has become almost legendary. It is based on the idea that if you examine the money you spend on small things with unrelenting regularity over time, you'll see that it can add up to a fortune.

For me, the Latte Factor for many years was smoking. I probably spent $5 a day on cigarettes. Now let's do the math. Five dollars a day is $35 a week, or $150 a month. If instead that $150 a month was invested at a rate of 10 percent, this is what I could have had:

1 year = $1,885
2 years = $3,967
5 years = $11,616
10 years = $30,727
15 years = $62,171

30 years = $339,073

40 years = **$948,611**

Start to understand your money patterns. What do you spend your money on? When do you buy things that you don't need? Which stores can you not go into without buying something? Which people make you want to spend more money? What is your decision process before you buy something?

You could sit down and think about all these questions and really try to examine your spending habits and money patterns, but it would be largely subjective and you are likely to miss critical pieces of information. The reason is because we are surprisingly unaware of many of our habits, especially in the areas of personal finance.

The best way to examine your money patterns is to keep a spending journal for a few months. Get yourself a small notebook that you can take with you wherever you go, and write down everything you spend money on. Everything. This will allow you to identify patterns, and will also allow you to pinpoint leaks in your financial life. It doesn't matter how big a boat is, a small leak will sink that boat over time. You need to find out exactly what the leaks are in your financial life so that you can repair them.

Savers and Spenders

Looking at your money patterns, you may be tempted to say, "Some people are savers and some people are spenders. I'm a spender! It's just who I am." I don't subscribe to this theory that some people are savers and other people are spenders, that this is just who they are and there is nothing they can do about it.

Some people have made themselves savers and other people have made themselves spenders. There is no gene that determines spending habits. We are not born savers or spenders. These are habits that are acquired with practice, and new habits can be acquired by practicing different types of behaviors.

Saving is not a dirty word. It may not be cool to save, but that's because the people that decide what is cool and what is not in our society have a vested interest in getting you to continuously consume.

You and I will never be financially free unless we begin to save. Developing the habit of saving is as important to your financial life as breathing is to your physical life. Perhaps you have been saving for years or perhaps you have never saved a single dollar. Whatever the case may be, decide today to become a saver.

The Essential Tool

The time to start saving money is as soon as you start earning money. As I was writing this book, I interviewed many people and discussed their perspectives on money, wealth, spending, saving, and investing. One of the questions I asked them was "What one piece of financial advice would you give to young people?" The answer I got in reply over and over again was, "Save . . . and start saving early."

In my teenage years I worked many small part-time jobs,

and I always saved a large portion of what I earned. Over time I began to notice that if I did not have a plan to save a certain amount, I would spend it all.

The only way to save money is to spend less than you earn. The average American spends 106 percent of his or her annual income annually. It is impossible under these circumstances to save and become financially free. You will never become financially free unless you learn how to control your expenses. Controlling your expenses and saving go hand in hand.

In order to control your expenses, you need a plan. This leads us to the most basic and essential tool in your efforts to become more financially free with every passing month. This tool is commonly referred to as a budget, and uncommonly employed. Less than 10 percent of Americans have and use a budget. Even more surprising is that a similarly small percentage of small businesses have and use a budget.

You need a budget. Without a budget your efforts to create and maintain the habits necessary to achieve your financial dreams will be threatened at every turn.

In the next chapter I am going to share with you one of my first budgets. I spent only $330 a week. With a quick glance you will notice I didn't have a car payment. You see, I didn't have a car until I was thirty. How did I get around? Public transport and the occasional taxi. Yes, it took a little longer, but that forced me to become a better manager of my time. This time on the bus or the train each day gave me an opportunity to think about life, and time to think about life is important to me. It's one of the parts of my day that I enjoy the most.

You will also notice that I didn't have a category for clothes. For five years I only bought clothes when I needed them. If you put a monthly category for clothes in your budget, you will buy clothes monthly. There is nothing wrong with having nice clothes, but if you had to choose between having less clothes and one day being completely financially free, which would you choose? You know what I am choosing.

What Do You Really Need?

The truth is, we need very little—food, clothing, and shelter. In their most basic forms, these are our legitimate needs. The important words here are "basic forms." Most of us enjoy food, clothing, and shelter many levels above anything that could be described as basic. Even when I challenged myself not to buy any clothes for a whole year, my wardrobe was still way above anything that could be described as basic—and nobody knew that I had not bought clothes in a year.

The sense of entitlement in our culture has gotten out of control, and as a result we have identified a great many things as needs that quite simply are not. The difference between want and need has been grossly distorted. You don't need anything "designer" and you don't need anything "luxury." This may sound boring, but being broke is boring . . . and there is nothing boring about having millions of dollars.

Confucius observed, "He who needs least has most."

The truth is, we don't really need that much. We want a lot of things, but that is different. What is it that you really need that you don't already have?

I would like a couple of Hugo Boss suits, but I don't need them. In fact, I can't remember the last time I really needed something. I've been sitting here thinking for about ten minutes and I cannot recall when I last genuinely needed something, which means it cannot have been that pressing.

If you are going to make this journey, create financial freedom, it is critically important that you get in touch with how little you actually need. It will be one of the greatest lessons you ever learn.

The key to each of the four stages of your financial life is to live within your means. The key to Stage One of your financial life is to live *below* your means. By living below your means, you are setting up your financial life.

It would seem the keys to living below your means are recognizing how little you really need and remembering that stuff is just stuff. Wander around your home and look at all the things you have that you don't need, that you never use, that you spent your hard-earned money on, that you thought were important at the time. Many of these are now just collecting dust or, worse, require your time and effort to dust them.

I was astounded recently to learn more about the self-storage business in the United States. First, let's think about what you put in self-storage. Extra stuff. Your garage is full and your basement is likely full of extra stuff, so the extra, extra stuff goes into self-storage. Many years ago a friend of mine told me he was going to open a self-storage facility. I thought he was crazy. But it only took him three months to get full occupancy, and the facility has remained more than 98 percent occupied ever since.

In the United States today, the self-storage business is larger than the motion picture business. That's right. I was astounded when I first heard it.

Stuff is just stuff. The quicker you learn to clearly decipher between what is essential and what is nonessential, the more likely you are to respect your hard-earned money and grow to become truly financially free.

Set your budget and live within your means. When you go shopping, before you buy anything, ask yourself, "Do I really need this?" The answer will almost always be "No!" That doesn't mean you should never buy things that you want. You should, and we will talk more about that. But getting really clear about what you need is an important learning experience in the quest for financial freedom.

When you consider how very hard most people work, and how little most people get paid for their work, it baffles me how readily most people waste their money on frivolous expenditures.

There Are Sacrifices to Be Made

Life and business require us to allocate scarce resources. Your time, money, energy, and attention are some of the scarce resources you are responsible for managing and allocating.

The allocation of these resources is usually simply a matter of saying yes to some things and no to others. But in a world where people are told they can have it all, we have trouble saying no to anything. It is little wonder then that most people are always short of time and money.

The only way to say no to something is to have a deeper *yes*. If you don't work out what your deeper *yes* is in the area of personal finance, you will never be able to say no to the things you need to say no to. I would like to suggest that you make financial freedom your deeper yes. Once you do, and identify what that means for you, you will find it much more manageable to say no to the things that get in the way of your financial freedom.

If you are clear about your deeper yes in the area of personal finance, next time you are thinking of buying a new pair of jeans or another pair of shoes that are not really a necessity, you will realize that you are making a choice between the jeans or shoes and $1 million, $3 million, or $5 million at retirement. You cannot have both. Life is about allocating scarce resources.

This is the time to make sacrifices. If you are consumed with external appearances, you are not going to make it. Most people are more concerned with looking financially successful than they are in *being* financially successful. But if you scratch just below the surface of most people's lives, you'll discover that they have little or no savings, little or no net worth, and are heavily burdened with consumer debt. But they look good.

It may not be sexy to drive an old beat-up car when you are twenty-five, but it is sexy to have $50 million when you are fifty. Living at home for a couple of years after school is not sexy, but it could set you up financially for life.

If you let your ego rule your financial life, you will end up in poverty.

These first eight years of your financial odyssey are a time of sacrifice. Your friends won't understand, but ask some people who are retired if they wish they had saved more when they were working, if they wish they had taken the time to put together a real financial plan, if they wish they had started saving earlier, and more than 99 percent will say that they do.

Ask the same people what their number one concern is at this time in their life, and you will discover firsthand what dozens of surveys have learned. The number one concern among the retired is that they will outlive their money. At a time in their life when they should be able to relax, and enjoy life and each other, most retired people worry more about money than at any other time in their lives.

Sacrifice is the seed that yields the fruit of financial success. You must ask yourself: "Am I willing to make the sacrifices necessary to achieve financial freedom?"

And while you are answering that question, consider the plight of the many immigrants who arrive in a country with little or nothing and proceed to build wealth way beyond most people who were born to that country. Immigrants in New York and Sydney, Paris and London, are sleeping six to a room, working double shifts, and leap-frogging the educated and entitled of my generation and yours, because they are willing to make sacrifices to build wealth and create a bigger future for themselves and their families.

Small sacrifices lead to huge rewards. You won't mind that you wore cheaper shoes, had fewer outfits, or didn't have your luxury coffee every day when you are free to decide if you want to go to work or not.

Have Fun with It

I have talked a lot about how difficult this is going to be. I keep mentioning commitment, discipline, and sacrifice. These are real and important, but in time you will begin to enjoy this journey toward your financial dreams.

Two ways I have learned to infuse fun into the process is with Zero Dollar Days and my Guilt-Free Money.

A Zero Dollar Day is exactly what it sounds like. This is a day when I try not to spend a single dollar—not in cash, not on my credit card, and not on my debit card. Zero. Nothing. Nada.

It's not easy. You'll want to make sure you have enough gas in your car the night before a Zero Dollar Day or that can do you in right there. Pack your lunch. Avoid the myriad of financial temptations, large and small, that stalk you around every corner in our modern world.

Try it. It can be one way to inject a little bit of entertainment into the process. Challenge your friends and family to have Zero Dollar Days too.

The other way I distract myself from the many disciplines and sacrifices I am making in order to gain financial freedom is with Guilt-Free Money. What is it? A certain amount of money each month that I can spend on anything I want. Anything.

At first this was as little as $50, but there is something psychologically liberating about being able to say to yourself, "I can spend this on anything I want!"

Of course, at first I wanted to buy all sorts of things, but these days my favorite things to buy are stocks in great companies.

Learn About Money

Continuous learning is a quality you always find in those who excel in their chosen field. If you want to excel in your quest for financial freedom, I would encourage you to be constantly learning about money and investing. Every day I read the financial pages of at least one major newspaper. This has been a habit of mine for more than a decade now. I also have an insatiable appetite for books like the one you are reading right now. I read them (often more than once), I listen to them in audiobook form when I am driving, and I discuss their ideas with my friends and colleagues to get different perspectives.

I have learned a great deal from financial books, the business pages of newspapers, and from magazines and seminars. But I have also learned an awful lot about money and myself by observing other people and their attitudes toward money.

I may not have been academically gifted in school, but I have always loved learning, and I suspect that since school, I have learned an awful lot more than most of my peers. So as we come to the close of this chapter about getting started and the basics of your financial life, I would like to encourage you to make learning about money a daily or weekly habit.

Now it is time to explore the four stages of your financial life.

CHAPTER FIVE

RIGHT NOW—STAGE ONE OF YOUR FINANCIAL LIFE

Building tremendous wealth really is not that difficult and does not require that you earn incredible amounts of money. But it does require time and patience, so the earlier you start the better. Remember the dripping faucet. Just turn your financial faucet on to a drip. You cannot change the past, so whether you are fifteen or fifty-five—start today.

If you are an early starter, you are at a massive advantage, as you will soon discover. Most young people say, "I am too young to be serious about money—this is my time to have fun!" And before you know it, they are playing catch-up.

If you are a late starter, don't get discouraged. You are at a disadvantage, but every week that you allow to pass will place you at a greater disadvantage. I will be honest with you. If you are a late starter, you will not be able to achieve what an early starter can, but you shouldn't let what you can't do interfere with what you can do.

Regardless of your age, if you follow the guidance of this book, your financial future will be significantly brighter than your financial past, and if you are starting early enough, you will achieve the kind of financial freedom that most people think is only for other people who are smarter than they are, luckier than they are, or earn more money than they do.

Why Aren't More People Financially Free?

One of the most powerful abilities human beings possess is the ability to desire. You can desire food, sex, money, possessions, love, and many other things. We all place the focus of our desire on different things from time to time, and what we place our focused desire on will always increase in our lives.

The problem is that most people have lost their ability to focus their desire. Our desire is more distracted than it is focused. A man sees a beautiful woman and he desires her. Then he sees some food that is appealing, and he desires it. He passes a bar and he desires a drink. He gets home, and he desires to collapse in front of the television. Desire is a wonderful thing, but it must remain our servant in order to be useful.

Desire is like money, a horrible master but a wonderful servant.

It is important that we acknowledge that we are in control of our desires. We can direct them at will and act on them at will. We can also redirect them when we sense that our desires have set themselves on something that will not help us achieve our hopes, dreams, and the very best for ourselves and our families.

Desire must be directed; otherwise our desires will run to whatever distracts them in the moment. And when our desire is spread too thin, it loses its power. It is also important to note that your desire does not know whether it is focused on something that is good for you or not. So it is important that you direct your desire to the things that are best for you, because your desire will act the same when focused on things that are good for you as it does when focused on things that will lead to your destruction. Whatever you focus your desire on will increase in your life, good or bad.

The reason more people are not financially free is because few people ever genuinely focus their desire on financial freedom. Most people think about it from time to time and say to themselves, "That would be nice!" But they have more desire for an ice cream or a new pair of shoes than they do for financial freedom. And, of course, they end up with what they place their focused and intense desires on: in this case, an ice cream and a new pair of shoes.

Desire is incredibly powerful. Whatever you place your mental attention on will increase in your life. If you really want to be financially free one day, then you need to start to focus your desire on financial freedom.

Two things are required to become financially free: desire and a plan. Napoleon once wrote, "Those who fail to plan can plan to fail." The same is true in our quest for financial freedom. I cannot give you the desire; you must stir it up within yourself. I can, however, help you with the plan, so let's get started.

Right Now: Stage One of Your Financial Life

The plan in Stage One is to develop the habit of saving. The core of Stage One is an eight-year savings plan. I will lay before you three plans now—good, better, and best. But you have to choose the one that is right for you. If you cannot commit to it, then there is no point choosing it. Keep in mind that even the good plan is considerably better than what 90 percent of people accomplish.

Let's explore the three options.

The First Eight Years

If you left school at eighteen years old, applied for a job at McDonald's, and applied yourself to a career with the company, this is what the first eight years of your career might look like with regards to roles and responsibilities and income.

TABLE 1—INCOME

Year	Age	Position	Monthly/Annual	After Tax
1	18	Crew	$1,655/$19,864	$19,103
2	19	Crew Trainer	$1,820/$21,840	$20,786
3	20	Front Counter Zone Manager	$2,250/$27,000	$25,166
4	21	Front Counter Zone Manager	$2,708/$32,500	$29,841
5	22	Drive-thru Zone Manager	$3,125/$37,500	$34,091
6	23	Drive-thru Zone Manager	$3,333/$40,000	$36,216
7	24	Grill Zone Manager	$3,583/$43,000	$38,766
8	25	Grill Zone Manager	$3,833/$46,000	$41,598

TABLE 2—BUDGET EXAMPLE

Category	Monthly	Annual
Rent	$325	$3,900
Utilities	$100	$1,200
Travel	$175	$2,100
Phone	$30	$360
Food and Household Supplies	$400	$4,800
Entertainment	$300	$3,600
Extras	$100	$1,200
	$1,430	**$17,160**

OPTION ONE—GOOD

If you choose to pursue Option One in the Right Now stage, the goal will be to save 10 percent of every paycheck, no exceptions. Option One will lead you to a nest egg of $32,369 during the course of this eight-year savings plan.

You will have saved an average of $3,237 a year. Even if this is the only saving you ever do, you will be well provided for in retirement. If you invest that $32,369 and leave it invested until you are sixty-five—earning an average return of 10 percent—at sixty-five you will have $1,456,609. Less than 3 percent of Americans retire with more than a million dollars. You'll do better . . . and all because you had the discipline to save for eight years.

TABLE 3

OPTION ONE—GOOD
SAVE 10 PERCENT OF YOUR AFTER-TAX
INCOME FOR EIGHT YEARS

Year/Age	After-Tax Pay	% of Pay Saved	Annual Savings	7%/$ Return Investment	Total Savings	Monthly Spending
1/18	$19,103	10%	$1,910	$134	$2,044	$1,430
2/19	$20,786	10%	$2,079	$288	$4,411	$1,559
3/20	$25,166	10%	$2,516	$485	$7,411	$1,887
4/21	$29,841	10%	$2,984	$727	$11,122	$2,238
5/22	$34,091	10%	$3,409	$1,017	$15,548	$2,556
6/23	$36,216	10%	$3,621	$1,341	$20,510	$2,716
7/24	$38,766	10%	$3,876	$1,707	$26,093	$2,907
8/25	$41,598	10%	$4,159	$2,117	$32,369	$3,109
	$245,567	10% Avg	$24,564	18/6		$32,369

OPTION TWO—BETTER

If you are willing to make a few more sacrifices, you may be able to save 20 percent of your income during the first eight years of your financial odyssey. It may sound like a lot, but I hope in the rest of this chapter to convince you that it is possible.

Needless to say, if you save twice as much, you will end up with twice as much. That's $61,357 after eight years . . . and $2,761,065 to retire with.

TABLE 4

OPTION TWO—BETTER
SAVE 20 PERCENT OF YOUR AFTER-TAX
INCOME OVER EIGHT YEARS

Year/Age	After-Tax Pay	% of Pay Saved	Annual Savings	7%/$ Return Investment	Total Savings	Monthly Spending
1/18	$19,103	10%	$1,910	$134	$2,044	$1,430
2/19	$20,786	12%	$2,494	$288	$4,411	$1,524
3/20	$25,166	14%	$3,523	$555	$8,489	$1,803
4/21	$29,841	17%	$5,072	$949	$14,510	$2,064
5/22	$34,091	20%	$6,818	$1,492	$22,820	$2,272
6/23	$36,216	23%	$8,329	$2,180	$33,329	$2,323
7/24	$38,766	25%	$9,691	$3,011	$46,031	$2,422
8/25	$41,598	27%	$11,312	$4,014	$21,357	$2,523
	$245,567	20% Avg	$49,149		$61,357	

OPTION THREE—BEST

This is the budget and savings plan that I followed from ages eighteen to twenty-five. I admit it is not for the faint of heart. This plan requires serious discipline and commitment.

Following this plan requires living on about $330 a week, or $1,430 a month, which I think we will all agree is not much. But it is possible, and there are many people who live on much less—not to mention the more than 2 billion people on this planet who live on less than $2 per day, or $14 a week, or $730 a year.

Follow this plan and you will amass $135,326 in your first eight years and be ready to retire at sixty-five with an incredible $6,089,620. All because you had the courage, foresight, and discipline to commit to a radical savings plan for eight years of your young life.

TABLE 5

OPTION THREE—BEST

LIVE ON $1,430 A MONTH FOR 8 YEARS

(THE ULTIMATE STAGE ONE SAVINGS PLAN)

Year/Age	After-Tax Pay	% of Pay Saved	Annual Savings	7%/$ Return Investment	Total Savings	Monthly Spending
1/18	$19,103	10%	$1,910	$134	$2,044	$1,430
2/19	$20,786	17.45%	$3,626	$397	$6,067	$1,430
3/20	$25,166	31.84%	$8,006	$985	$15,058	$1,430
4/21	$29,841	42.55%	$12,681	$1,941	$29,680	$1,430
5/22	$34,091	49.75%	$16,931	$3,262	$49,873	$1,430
6/23	$36,216	52.63%	$19,056	$4,825	$73,754	$1,430
7/24	$38,766	55.85%	$21,606	$6,675	$102,035	$1,430
8/25	$41,598	58.82%	$24,438	$8,853	$135,326	$1,430
		44% Avg	$108,254		$135,326	

The Assumptions

All the illustrations above are based on the assumption that you will earn a 7 percent return during the first eight years and a 10 percent return from year nine to retirement. Now, some people may argue that these returns are not realistic; however, if for the last twenty years you had purchased McDonald's shares each month with the amount you saved, your average annual return would have been more than 10 percent in growth and more than 3 percent in dividends (which the company has paid every year since 1976).

If, on the other hand, you had simply bought an S&P 500 index fund, historically your return would have been 11.5 percent, including dividends.

Needless to say, in the market there will be times when you will make much more (for example the 18 percent and 20 percent increases during the 1980s) and times when the value of your shares will decline (as they did in 2008).

And even if you realized a return of 8 percent or 9 percent instead of the 10 percent I used for the illustrations, you would still be in a better position than most people. Assumptions are assumptions, and they are necessary to illustrate the model. But if you don't like the assumptions, by all means perform the illustration with your own assumptions. Just don't let the assumptions become an excuse not to start, and start today. If you feel more comfortable with a lower rate of expected return, you can use any online savings calculator to explore other options.

Start Early and Start Strong

As you have no doubt already figured out, starting early creates a powerful and compounding advantage. Take, for instance, the three options presented in the preceding pages. Option One would net you $1,456,609 at sixty-five if you committed to the plan between the ages of eighteen and twenty-five, Option Two would net you $2,761,065, and Option Three would net you $6,089,620.

But if instead of beginning at eighteen, you waited until you were twenty-eight to begin Stage One, the difference would be enormous.

Option One. Instead of $1,456,609 at sixty-five, you would have just $642,117, even though you saved the same amount of money.

Option Two. Instead of $2,761,065, you would have just $1,217,163.

Option Three. Instead of $6,089,620, you would have just $2,684,516.

The lesson here is start early, and start strong. The earliest you can start is today. If you are already twenty-eight or thirty-eight or fifty-eight, there is no point lamenting the past. Begin today. I am not going to sugarcoat the situation: You would have been much better off if you had started saving long ago. But if you do start saving today, your future will still be bigger and better and brighter than if you don't.

If you are a college student, or about to begin college in the next couple of years, you may be thinking, "I cannot begin to earn or save that kind of money while I am in college." That is a fair observation. But with a college education, you will be able to earn much more than the McDonald's employee I have outlined above, and if you stick to the plan, you will more than catch up over time.

So set this book down now and schedule a time to work on your budget. You can sketch something out quickly, but to really get the numbers right you will probably need to find your old bills and new bills and take a close look at the various inflows and outflows of money in your life.

Stage One is all about making a plan and sticking to the plan. It will be the most disciplined time of your financial life. It won't be easy, but it will be worthwhile. You will never regret getting this early start financially.

From here on, you will never have to save again, unless you choose to. Your retirement and your legacy will be secure. Now let's move on to Stage Two, where you will be able to enjoy the fruits of your financial efforts.

CHAPTER SIX

QUALITY OF LIFE—STAGE TWO OF YOUR FINANCIAL LIFE

Guidelines for Stage Two

Stage Two will run from age twenty-six until age sixty-five, or from the end of Stage One until retirement. The guidelines for Stage Two are very simple: Spend everything you earn. Save a bit if you want.

That's right, in this stage of your financial life you can spend everything you earn. You have done the hard yards, and now it is time to enjoy your money a little. If you followed what I laid out for you in Stage One, you will have changed your financial destiny, and very likely the financial destiny of your entire family for many generations to come.

Now, that does not mean that you have to spend everything you earn. And given that you have developed the habit of saving and investing, you have probably started to enjoy watching your money grow over time. You will probably continue to save some portion of your income—and I will lay out a few options later in this chapter—but I want to be abundantly clear in saying that if you spend everything you earn in Stage Two, from ages twenty-six to sixty-five, you will still be adhering to the plan perfectly.

What Have You Achieved So Far?

But before we press on in the quality of life stage, let's briefly recap what you have already achieved.

By the time you arrive at Stage Two of your financial life, you will have provided significant security for your retirement. But, more important, you will have developed an ability to delay gratification that will serve you not only in

The hard work is done. Follow the plan for Stage One and your retirement nest egg will be well formed and will continue to grow. Stage Two is all about enjoying the fruits of your labor, spending your money on the things that enrich your life, and enjoying the things of this world. Even if you do not save a penny in Stage Two, you will retire with several times what the average person retires with—an amount in the millions of dollars.

If you begin Stage One at eighteen, Stage Two will begin at twenty-six. If you begin Stage One at twenty-two (after college or as a late starter), this stage will begin at age thirty. And if you begin at any age after twenty-two, the quality of life stage will begin eight years after you begin Stage One.

financial matters, but also in your relationships, career, health and well-being, and in every other arena of your life. In addition to having nurtured this ability to delay gratification, you will have developed the discipline and respect for money necessary to ensure that you never become a financial slave.

How Much Is Enough?

This is the big question that you will need to ask and answer in Stage Two. When you arrive at this stage in your life, you will begin to have a much clearer idea of how much you really need. You will also have made many of the life choices that determine how much money we need. These decisions include where to live, whether or not to get married, and how many children you are going to have.

You are now moving into the middle of life, and it is time to answer this question: How much is enough? There are plenty of people who live on $50,000 or less each year. There are other people who feel they need ten times this amount.

So let's start to work out how much you need to live the life you imagine. In the previous chapter, we calculated what it would cost to purchase your basic financial freedom. But now let's dream a little and work out the cost of the lifestyle (and financial freedom in that lifestyle) that you envision for yourself and those you love.

Perhaps in this stage in your life you want to buy a home, take great vacations, be able to go on a shopping spree once a month, and drive a luxury car. What's important to you may not be important to the next person, so it is essential that you customize your vision of this quality of life stage of your financial odyssey.

I talked to one of my colleagues, Peter, about these very things and this is what he shared with me. These are the things he wants to enjoy in the quality-of-life stage, and how much he thinks they will cost.

"Well, I'd like to have a nice home. Nothing too big, just a
  nice family home that I enjoy spending time in."
Price: $400,000. Monthly mortgage payment: $2,500 (approx).

"I'd also like to take one great vacation each year with my
  wife and two children."
Price: $7,200, or $600 per month.

"I'd like to buy my wife nice gifts and I'd also like her to
  be able to go shopping from time to time and splurge."
Price: $750 per month.

"I'd like a BMW. I don't need a new one, but I have always
  wanted one and I think that would be a great dream to
  accomplish."
Price: $350 per month.

"It would be great to start a college fund for my children."
Price: $150 per month.

On top of all these, Peter has other regular expenses like food and gas, insurance, and property taxes. He estimates that these cost him on average $1,200 per month.

This brings his monthly total to $5,550 per month or $66,600 each year.

As we learned in the last chapter, with a modest return of 5 percent, Peter would need $1,322,000 invested to retire today and maintain this lifestyle he envisions. But Peter doesn't want to retire. He makes $55,000 a year and his wife makes $42,000 a year, and together they can very much enjoy the quality-of-life stage. As Peter's income increases, his wife would like to work three days a week and spend more time with the children, but that is still three or four years away.

I had the same conversation with several other friends and colleagues. Julia's annual number was only $42,000, which would require $840,000 invested to be financially free. Jamal's number was $51,000, which would require $1,020,000 invested to be financially free. And Michael, whose children are grown, arrived at an annual number of only $27,000. This would require only $540,000 invested.

I found a couple of things Michael said to be quite interesting. He said, "The older I get, the less interested I am in spending money. I would rather have a root canal than go shopping." So I asked him, "But wouldn't you like to retire early?" He replied, "Absolutely not. People look at me working here at the store, and I can see them thinking, 'Poor old man, working at McDonald's.' But I don't feel that way. First of all, I am not old. I am only fifty-four. Secondly, I like being here and helping people—our customers and the other employees. I like talking to the young people about what is happening in their lives, and encouraging them to live with passion."

It was then no surprise to learn that Michael did not have a financial concern in the world. He had been saving all his life, lives a simple life, and his savings provide more than enough for him to live on—even before his paycheck from McDonald's.

Peter imagines a life where he needs more than twice what Michael needs, but I cannot imagine anyone could be more content than Michael is. That doesn't make Peter bad or wrong, but it does make the wisdom of Michael's simple life lead me to pause and reflect.

How much is enough? Only you can decide. If you are married, then you and your spouse need to decide together. But whatever number you come up with for annual living expenses, multiply it by twenty and that is the cost of financial freedom in that lifestyle.

It's important to know how much would secure your basic financial freedom (as we did in the last chapter), but it is also important to work out how much money you would need to be financially free in the lifestyle you imagine for yourself. Not everyone desires great financial fortunes. Some people desire a simple life in a quiet place doing things that cost little or nothing, such as reading, gardening, fishing, or volunteering. Others desire to live a life filled with luxury cars, private jets, multiple homes, fine clothes, traveling the world, and eating at all the best restaurants. While still another person may love his work and dread the idea of not working. What appeals to one person is positively repulsive to another. You must decide for yourself. What life would you like to lead and how much money do you need to live it?

A Big Decision

Stage Two of your financial life—the quality-of-life stage—will be filled with many life-directing decisions surrounding career and relationships, where to live, and how to live. But the biggest decision you will make regarding money in the second stage of your financial life is the choice between lifestyle and wealth.

Most people make this decision unconsciously. Many never get to make this decision, because they are just constantly in survival mode financially. Live from month to month, and more often than not toward the end of the month there will be more month left than there is money.

Follow the plan I have laid out for Stage One of your financial life and you will put yourself beyond this financial survival mode forever.

As you read in the opening of Chapter 2 about how a family could become the wealthiest in the world, you may have found it interesting but at the same time have no desire to build wealth on that scale or to be that family. Instead of building a billion-dollar family name, you may want to save and invest so that you can have an incredible lifestyle. That is for you to decide.

If you adhere to the plan laid out for Stage One of your financial life, then in Stage Two you can spend everything you earn. This of course presumes that you will not touch the nest egg you have set aside in Stage One. So, it is recommended that at the beginning of Stage Two you set aside at least a portion of your income for unexpected expenses. Expect the unexpected and you will rarely be disappointed when it comes to expenses. There is always going to be some expense that you did not expect. Anticipate that and put some money aside so you don't have to dig into your nest egg.

The beginning of Stage Two is also a perfect time to save for lifestyle adjustments that you already foresee. For some people this may involve buying a home, for others it might be taking a few years off work to have and raise children, and for others still it may mean sending their children to the best schools and colleges. If you foresee these things in your life, then now is the time to start planning for them financially.

In the case of children, few people can honestly claim that they could not save $1 each day for their child's future. If you start saving $1 each day when your child is born, and invest it with a 10 percent return, on your child's twenty-first birthday you will be able to gift him or her with $26,395. Push yourself and set aside $3 a day for your child and that number increases to $79,185. Go crazy and set aside $7 a day and that number becomes $184,765.

Now, perhaps your dream is to buy a home. You may be tempted to take the money saved in Stage One and use it for a deposit. That would be a mistake. A big mistake. In fact you would be breaking the one cardinal law of the plan I am laying before you. So how do you gather a deposit to buy a home?

You have developed the habit of saving and investing, and if you are willing to press on for a little longer, the rewards can be enormous. Once I had turned twenty-six and completed Stage One, I decided to press on with saving, and I committed myself to another five-year savings plan. Of course, my salary was continuing to rise, so I was able to enjoy a better lifestyle while at the same time continuing to save.

The optional savings plan I would like to lay before you now is not necessarily for retirement. You may decide to use it to buy a home in the future, or to put your children through college. You may desire it simply to increase your financial peace of mind.

Regardless of what you want the money for eventually, I will lay before you three optional five-year savings plans. I will assume that you will begin them in the first five years of Stage Two. This would be from ages twenty-six to thirty if you began Stage One at eighteen, and from ages thirty to thirty-four, if you began Stage One at age twenty-two, after college.

For ease of understanding, let us assume that you enter Stage Two earning $50,000, as you could reasonably expect to do as a store manager at McDonald's. Let us also assume, for simplicity's sake, that for the five years of this optional savings plan, your salary will not increase but will remain at $50,000. If you stick to the same spending habits you have in Stage One for five more years, this is what you could save for a deposit on a home:

Option One—Good. In this case, you would be saving
   10 percent of your after-tax pay, or $4,400 a year. After
   five years, with a return of 10 percent, you would have
   $29,548.

Option Two—Better. In this case, you would be saving
  20 percent of your after-tax pay, or $8,800 a year. After
  five years, with a return of 10 percent, you would have
  $59,096.
Option Three—Best. In this case, you would still be spending only $1,430 a month and saving $26,844 a year.
  After five years, with a return of 10 percent, you would
  have $178,929.

These are lifestyle choices that we have to make for ourselves. Even after an extra five years of saving, you will still
be only thirty-one years old, and the very best years of your
life will be ahead of you. The only difference is that you will
be able to enjoy them in a way that most people cannot
because they are worrying about money or having to save
at incredible levels to ensure a future for themselves and their
families.

If, on the other hand, you are more interested in building
wealth than you are in lifestyle, then you are now perfectly set
up to take that quest to the next level.

Perhaps you decide to follow *Option One—Good,* but instead of using the money you save over those five years for
a deposit on a home, you continue to rent. You continue to
invest the $29,548 from the five-year savings plan at a return
of 10 percent. By the time you are sixty-five, that $29,548
will have grown to $964,407.

Or perhaps you decide to follow *Option Two—Better,* but
instead continue to invest those funds. You continue to invest the $59,096 from the five-year savings plan at a return of

10 percent. By the time you are sixty-five, that $59,096 will have grown to $1,928,814.

Finally, you may decide to follow *Option Three—Best* but continue to invest that money. You continue to invest the $178,929 from the five-year savings plan at a return of 10 percent. By the time you are 65, that $178,929 will have grown to $5,840,001, or $15,809,125 at seventy-five, or $42,795,958 by the time you are eighty-five. Imagine the legacy of good you could leave behind for your family and for people you will never know.

You decide: wealth or lifestyle?

One Step Further

Once developed, the habit of saving should never be squandered. I will save for the rest of my life. The habit is so deeply ingrained that to throw it away would seem like a terrible waste. With each passing year I am learning to enjoy the money I earn a little more, but I remain deeply committed to my financial dreams and goals.

Imagine you saved $1,000 a month every month from the age of twenty-six to retirement at age of sixty-five. Assuming the same rate of return as we have in all our previous examples, the result would be more than $6.3 million.

Sure $1,000 a month is a lot at twenty-six, but the next year you earn a little bit more it will seem like a little bit less. When you are thirty-five, if you have kept investing in yourself and kept adding value to your organization, you will be earning much more than you did at twenty-six, and the $1,000 a month will not seem so much. At forty-five, it will seem like very little, but you will see it multiplying before your very eyes into a legacy that will change the financial destiny of your family forever.

You Decide

Stage Two is all about enjoying your income. I am a huge advocate of saving and in my own life often take it a little further than most people are comfortable with, but I am not suggesting that you just save and save and save, and never enjoy the fruits of your labor. Not at all. I am simply suggesting that you get the power of time and multiplication of money on your side.

If you follow the Stage One plan and decide to spend every penny you earn in Stage Two—nobody will be happier for you than I will be. If you decide to press on with saving in Stage Two and build wealth beyond your wildest imaginings—I will be equally happy for you. It's up to you.

What is important to me may not be important to you. What is important to you may not ignite passion and purpose in me. One way is not right and the other wrong. One is not better than the other. They are just different. Only you can decide the path you are called along. But choose. Don't just aimlessly stumble down one. Decide.

Beyond the Money

Now that you have a money plan and you are working your money plan, you can enjoy this quality-of-life stage as most people never get an opportunity to. Throughout this book I have tried to be as honest with you as possible, even when that means delivering difficult truths. It is time for another moment of honesty. There are many more important things in life than money, but without money these things are difficult to really enjoy.

You are now in the middle of life. This stage of life is where you will form your most significant relationships, find your way to the job that really engages you, buy a home, perhaps have a family, and learn to provide for your future by investing. Most people spend these forty years of their lives worrying about money, but that will not be you if you take what you read about Stage One seriously. Most people in this second stage of their financial life are struggling to save for retirement and realizing that they have left it too late. Others are spending all they earn, but did not save as outlined in Stage One, and with every passing day they are one step closer to their financial doom. Many people have a negative net worth, and many more could not survive a couple of months if they lost their job today. But not you—you can spend all you earn in Stage Two of your financial life, confident that you are on a solid financial footing. Or you can continue to save a portion of all you earn, changing the financial DNA of your family line forever and building wealth beyond most people's imagining.

The truth is, the most important things in life have nothing to do with money. But without money your ability to enjoy the best things money cannot buy will be limited.

Do you really want to be working all the time while your

children are growing up? Do you really want to be worrying about money when you are on vacation with the one you love? Do you really want to be stuck in a job you hate because you are so financially insecure that you cannot afford the risk of a career change?

In the second half of this chapter we will discuss five aspects of this period in our lives: relationships, home, career, investing, and health. It is in these areas that you will face many of the biggest decisions you will make in your life.

Relationships—To Love and Be Loved

There is no point having a fabulous life if you don't have people to share it with. In fact, I don't think a fabulous life is possible without great people in it. In the same way, there is no point building incredible wealth if you have no one to share it with. It is the sharing of wealth that multiplies the joy it brings.

Let us consider three types of relationships: dating and marriage; children; and friends.

DATING AND MARRIAGE

It is in this stage of life that most people get married, and half of those will get divorced. Few things will impact your financial health and your ability to achieve financial independence like your partner's attitude toward money. In selecting someone to spend the rest of our lives with, there are many factors to consider, and attitude toward money is one of them. Not because money is the most important thing in the world or in a relationship, but because differing attitudes toward it are the number one cause of tension in relationships.

A person's attitude toward money, saving, investing, and financial independence tells you a lot more about the person than merely how he or she thinks about money. Tell me about your attitude toward money and I will know about your ability to delay gratification, what you value, and how capable you are of envisioning the future.

Great relationships require all the talents you will build through the discipline of saving, investing, and creating financial independence. If you marry someone who is unable to delay gratification, this will lead to friction in a hundred different ways in your relationship. If you marry someone who values very different things from what you value, this will be the source of constant tension. And if you marry someone who is unwilling to envision a better future and work toward it, then you are going to feel that your potential is being stifled.

If you are married already, then you have to do your best to reconcile whatever differences may exist in each of these areas. They are not impossible obstacles. All of these good habits can be acquired along the way. None of us is born with innate abilities to delay gratification, value the right things, and envision an abundant future. These are habits of the mind and spirit that are developed by disciplining ourselves.

If you are not already married, then it may be useful to consider these questions when you are dating.

1. Does this person help me celebrate my best self?
2. Is this person capable of delaying gratification?

3. How are our attitudes toward money and saving different?

CHILDREN

Once you have found the person you want to build a life with, I hope you are further blessed with the joy of children. If you follow the guidance outlined in Stage One, you will be able to spend more time with your children than the great majority of people can, and you will have a valuable set of skills to pass on to them.

The wealthy are notorious for not giving their children the opportunities necessary to develop a healthy respect for money and career. They are also notorious for not educating their children about the laws of money. And they rarely communicate to their children the incredible opportunity they have to make a contribution to society independent of the burdens of making a living. As a result, too often the children of the wealthy waste their lives and squander the wealth that their parents worked so hard to achieve.

Many of life's greatest lessons can be learned on a football field, in a library, or by studying the laws of money.

If you build wealth in the way I am outlining in this book, you will be able to teach your children to be good stewards of your family's financial resources. Warren Buffett's children will tell you that not until late in their lives did he teach them anything about money. He gave them all shares in his company, which they proceeded to sell. But he did not counsel them what to do with the shares. He did not counsel them that using the shares as collateral, they could have taken a loan for the houses they bought with the money. Stunning as it may seem, the greatest investor in history taught his children very little about money. Don't let the same be said of you and your children.

Knowledge of how money and investing work is one of the greatest areas of practical wisdom you can school your children in. Unless our educational systems change, they will not pick up these things in high school or college or even, amazingly, business school. As a result, knowledge of the laws of money provides those who have it with a distinct advantage over their peers. As we have seen very clearly in Stage One, two people could be earning exactly the same income; one saves nothing, while the other saves $100 a week. The second person will retire with countless millions of dollars more than the former.

It is much better to teach your children the laws of money than to give them money. In fact, inherited wealth is one of the great evils of our time. It creates a sense of entitlement, stifles ambition, innovation, and creativity, and often leads those who receive it to miss the path that was intended for them.

The reason, it seems, is that through the process of building wealth we are also likely to build the character necessary to manage that wealth in healthy ways. But when we pass that wealth on to others, we cannot also pass on the character we built while accumulating the wealth. For this reason, if we are going to be wealthy and have children, and pass our wealth onto our children, then we must proactively seek ways to help them develop the character necessary to be good stewards of the wealth we intend to entrust to them.

Done properly, such education will also provide many opportunities to teach our children about relationships, the value of opportunities, the power of dreams, the importance of making a contribution, the role discipline plays in our lives, and the universal principles of success.

Friends

Our friends have an enormous impact on our quality of life and are enormously influential when it comes to our attitudes and behaviors toward money.

If your friends are voracious consumers, then it will take an enormous amount of self-discipline for you to stay on the path toward financial freedom. If your friends are committed to saving, investing, and the pursuit of financial independence, then when you are having a moment of weakness, you will be able to call upon their support to keep you strong.

The nature and quality of your friendships will determine what you spend most of your time talking and thinking about. Whatever we talk and think about increases in our lives. If you spend all your time talking about the latest shoes, handbags, cars, watches, and consumables in general, you will become a voracious consumer. If, on the other hand, you spend most of your time thinking and talking about saving, investing, and your dream of being financially independent, you will become a prolific saver and investor.

Friendships either help us celebrate our best selves or not. There is no middle ground. My father used to say that if I could find five true friends to make my way through this life with I would be truly blessed beyond measure.

It is great to have some money, and better not to have to worry about money. It is wonderful to be able to buy and enjoy things. It is fabulous to be saving and investing to create financial independence for yourself and to change the financial DNA of your family forever. But there is nothing better than investing in those few relationships with people who bring the best out of you, whether you have just experienced your greatest triumph or your biggest defeat. We all need people to do life with, and the higher the quality of people we attract to ourselves to form this inner circle, the richer our lives tend to be in every sense of the word.

No amount of money compares to the joy of loving and being loved. And yet money affords us the ability to enrich relationships with opportunities that make the adventure of life ever more enjoyable.

Home—A Sanctuary from the World

In *The Wizard of Oz* Dorothy woke up mumbling, "There's no place like home." It would seem that having a place and space of our own, somewhere to just be, a place where we belong, is critically important to our happiness as human beings. We do not necessarily need anything lavish or extravagant, though we may desire such. We simply need somewhere of our own. This place can take the form of a house or a condo in our adult life, and when we are children it takes the form of a bedroom. We all need a place to call home, and there is something immediately settling about arriving at that place.

The purchase of a home will likely be the largest single purchase of your life. I say "single purchase" because it is my hope that you spend much more buying stocks in great companies than you spend buying your home—but investing in stocks will consist of many smaller purchases over time. Buying a home is an enormous decision and one that should not be taken lightly.

When you are buying a home, there are a great many things to consider, such as where to buy, when to buy, how much to spend, how to finance the purchase, whether the home is close to good schools if you have or plan on having children, how far you will have to commute for work, and many others. Suffice it to say that this book is not solely about buying a home, and I would recommend you do your due diligence with more specific guides in all of these areas when the time comes. What I am primarily concerned with discussing here is how the purchase of a home could affect your goal of financial freedom and, more to the point, how you can go about purchasing a home in such a way that it does not threaten your financial freedom.

In Chapter 2 we discussed the seven unchanging laws of money. It is now time for us to turn our attention to the law that states, "Make your home an investment."

Very often when people buy a home, you will hear them say things like "It is a great investment." Or their family and friends will urge them on by saying, "It is a great investment." The assumption always seems to be that this enormous purchase is an investment. This is an assumption that needs to be challenged, and in order to do so, let us consider this question. What is an investment?

When I Google the question, I come up with more than 37,000,000 results, but the first one will work as a starting point for our conversation. It reads, "The investing of money or capital in order to gain profitable returns, as interest, income, or appreciation in value." This definition is accurate, but the world of investing is complex.

My brothers taught me growing up that an investment was something that produced a non-exertive stream of income. For example, if I buy some land and rent that land, the rent is non-exertive income. If I buy shares in McDonald's (MCD), I receive dividends. These dividends are non-exertive income. As I am writing these pages, the cost per share is $58.78, and the annual dividend is 3.74 percent. For every share I own I will receive $2.20 a year in dividends. Over twenty-five years these dividends will pay for the shares, and I will still have the shares, which will likely be worth significantly more than I paid for them. But when I go to work to make money, my paycheck is exertive income. If I do not exert, I don't get it.

This is the difference between non-exertive, or passive, and active income. Financial freedom is all about creating passive income. Passive income in the definition above comes from interest and income (dividends, for example). The third component—appreciation—does not produce passive income. You are required to sell the asset in order to get the money. This is a lower class of investment simply because of the nature of our goal—which is financial freedom. Ideally, I would like to help you create a situation where all you do is wait for the dividend and rent checks to arrive each month. Financial freedom is creating sufficient passive streams of income to cover your cost of living. I love dividend-paying stocks in world-class companies because they allow me to ensure passive flows of income and also take advantage of appreciation opportunities if I choose to. Now let us return to our discussion of a home as an investment.

A home can certainly fit into the third category—appreciation. But in order to get the money, you will have to sell the home. Do you want to have to sell the home that is full of a lifetime of memories just because you need the money to live on? I think in most cases the answer would be no, if there is another way. There is another way, so let's explore it.

WHAT IS A HOUSE?

If you had to choose between owning a castle and having a modest home but being financially free, I hope you would choose the latter. Whether we are buying a home or a new pair of shoes, we are always choosing between the purchase and financial freedom. It is unhealthy to become overly obsessive about this, but it is important to recognize that this is the choice being made. It is also important to realize that unless you become at least a little bit obsessed with financial freedom, you will never achieve it.

In the second stage of financial life, most people purchase a home. The great irony is that they tend to think of their homes as investments. And yet from the moment they purchase the home, they do nothing but spend money on it. After making the biggest so-called investment of their lives, they then spend the rest of their lives working to pay for this "investment." I prefer investments that work for me. I prefer investments that pay me. The most painful iteration of this situation I see is when I meet people who are stuck in a job or career that they despise but cannot escape because of the slavery of a mortgage.

So before we jump into purchasing a home, let us consider some fundamental questions. What is the purpose of a home? What sort of home do we really need? Is the slavery that a more extravagant home requires really worth it?

To guide us in this discussion, let us turn to a radically clear-thinking American of the nineteenth century, Henry David Thoreau. Allow me to share with you a handful of the briefest excerpts from his *Walden* reflections, in particular from his writings entitled "Where I Lived, and What I Lived For." I will offer them in their raw form, without additional comment at first, so that you can reflect on them in your own way.

"Consider first how slight a shelter is absolutely necessary."
"Many a man is harassed to death to pay the rent of a larger and more luxurious box . . . than he needs to live comfortably."
It is their dwellings "that keep them poor as long as they live."
"I am surprised to learn that most cannot name a dozen in their town who own their homes free and clear."
"And when a man has got his house, he may not be the richer but the poorer for it, and it may be that the house has got him."

"Our houses are such unwieldy property that we are often imprisoned rather than housed in them."

"Most men appear never to have considered what a house is, and are actually though needlessly poor all their lives because they think that they must have such a one as their neighbors have."

All in all, it seems to me that our home should be a comfortable place to rest and enjoy our family, friends, hobbies, and interests. It should be the place where we have the least anxiety in the world, a place where we can take a break from the constant pressure of modern life. With this in mind, it would seem to me that our home should embody the simplicity and efficiency of providing as much pleasure as possible while at the same time producing as little work and anxiety as possible.

WHAT IS THE REAL COST?

The real cost of anything is not what is on the price tag. In Chapter 4 we explored the question, "What's a dollar worth?" In the process we came to a better understanding of the real financial costs involved in buying a TV, or anything else for that matter. Every purchase costs much more than the sticker price, because in making that purchase you also surrender all future interest or dividends that you could have earned from that money if you had not spent it and had instead invested it. We then went on to explain that the real cost is not even financial, but rather a certain amount of time that you will have to keep working because a certain purchase will keep you one step (or several steps) away from being financially free.

Now let's explore the real costs of buying a home.

For example, let's say you buy a home for $400,000 with a deposit of $50,000. With an interest rate of 7 percent, to repay the loan of $350,000 over thirty years, your monthly payments would be $2,328.56. Over the course of the loan you will make payments totaling $838,281.60. Your total interest bill for this investment will be $488,281.60.

This of course does not take into account property taxes; regular maintenance, improvements, and upgrades; and monthly expenses such as utilities. Over time your property will appreciate, but when all these costs are taken into account, few people ever really make money on their homes.

Beyond these costs are more subtle costs that are worthy of our attention. You cannot put a price on worrying about whether or not you will be able to make the mortgage payment. You cannot put a price on the stress and anxiety of spending your weekends working on your house when you would rather be pursuing your passions and interests.

And the real cost of anything always has to include the opportunity that is lost because of the choice you make to acquire it. The opportunity cost of purchasing a house is all the things you could have done with that money if you had not bought that home, or if you had purchased something more affordable. Let me lay before you two examples.

Example One: Instead of purchasing a home, you rented one. Now let us assume that you could rent a home for $1,000 a month. Instead of spending $2,328.56 a month on a mortgage, you could invest the difference of $1,328.56. Even if your investment returned only a humble 7 percent, after thirty years you would have $1,620,805 from this investment alone. This is a lost opportunity and has to be considered.

Example Two: Instead of buying a home for $400,000, you purchased one for $250,000. You still place a deposit on the home of $50,000 as in the above example and your interest rate would still be 7 percent for thirty years. But now, instead of a monthly mortgage payment of $2,328.56, your payment would be just $1,330.60. If you invested the difference, or $997.96, each month for the thirty years and received a return of 7 percent, you would amass $1,217,482.

Beyond the money itself you have to also factor in that having an extra million dollars thirty years from now is going to afford you certain peace of mind and opportunities. What are these worth? Only you can decide.

By all means, I want you to have somewhere to call home, a place where you can rest and relax and be at peace with yourself and your life. But in the grand scheme of things I would rather you have a modest home and never have to worry about money.

Career

Many people get to a point in their thirties or forties when they wish they could change their career or start a business of their own, but because of their financial nearsightedness during the first stage of their financial lives, they are simply not able to. When they come to this realization, quiet desperation begins to set in for many. They smile and keep up appearances, but inside they are slowly dying. They keep consuming at financially suicidal rates because it makes them feel successful or they think that it is important . . . and in truth many of them never had anyone explain to them what I am explaining to you in these pages.

For you it will be different. Make the sacrifices you need to make in Stage One, and you will never be helplessly trapped in a job that is not for you. In the first stage, you may have to tolerate a job that you do not like, but to my way of thinking it is better to endure that for eight years than to be stuck in a rut for the rest of your working life.

In high school people talk a lot about what they are going to do when they get out. Our society seems obsessed with the question "What do you want to be when you grow up?" from as soon as we can walk and talk. But as I look back on my high school class of more than 150 students, it would seem that fewer than 10 percent of them are actually doing what they thought they would be doing. When we are young, in this first stage of our financial lives, we are still very much getting to know ourselves. Most people don't end up doing what they started out doing, and many of those who do don't keep working those jobs because they want to. They feel trapped.

Take the years of Stage One, ideally from ages eighteen to twenty-five, to work out what it is you really want to do. Don't jump around incessantly, and never quit your job before you have found your next one. But observe yourself. Consider what your strengths and weaknesses are professionally. Explore what you do and do not like doing. And as you approach the second stage of your financial life, make an effort to move in the direction of a job that compensates you and stimulates you in the ways that you desire.

If a bold move is required, make it. It may mean a financial setback initially, but in the long run, if you are doing something that you genuinely enjoy and that you feel is making a contribution, you will be more successful at it anyway. In most fields, this will in turn lead to more income. But even if it does not, you cannot put a price on the joy that comes from doing something you really enjoy. When you love who you are moving through life with and you love what you are doing, you can live without a lot of the superficial things money can buy. But when you don't have these two basics, when you don't love who you are moving through life with and you don't love what you are doing, all the money and possessions in the world are not enough to satisfy the emptiness you will feel inside.

Investing

Nobody cares more about your money than you do. It doesn't matter how good your financial advisors are, or how much you trust them—it is unlikely that they are going to lie awake worrying about your money for you. If they are going to lie awake worrying about someone's money, it will be their own. By the second stage of your financial life, you will have accumulated a significant amount of investable assets, and by the end of this second stage you will have accumulated investable assets that will stagger most people's imaginations. It is now critical that you begin to study investing. That doesn't mean you need an advanced finance and investing degree. It just means that you need to read books about investing, subscribe to an investing magazine, and familiarize yourself with the business and investing pages of the newspaper.

Investing is one of my interests, hobbies, and passions. I just enjoy it. It may not be that way for you, and it does not have to be. You do, however, need a basic knowledge of investing. You need to meet regularly with your financial advisor. And you need to keep an eye on your investments.

Visit *www.moneyclassroom.com* for a list of books that have changed my financial life.

Health

The biggest choice you will make in the quality-of-life stage is actually a hundred thousand small choices. Every day we choose between optimal health and disease. Somewhere in the middle is the very average and ordinary health that most of us experience. More and more, it seems a lot of people are always tired.

There is no point having money if you don't have the health to enjoy it, so if you have not been doing so up until now, start taking care of yourself.

Investing in yourself and your future capacity to earn means, above all, taking care of your health. The healthier you are, the harder and longer you will be able to work when that is what is required, and the more mental focus you will have.

I am not saying you have to become a gym rat, just suggesting that at the beginning or end of each day you take a long walk or go for a run. Every night I try to go for a walk. It doesn't matter how late I get home; this is an important part of my daily routine. Walking clears my mind. It allows me to reflect on the day that is ending and prepare for the next day.

The quality-of-life stage begins at twenty-six and ends at sixty-five if you follow this plan beginning at eighteen. Most people who have made it through this stage will tell you that this times flies. So enjoy it. If you are just getting started, pay your dues in Stage One, so that you can really enjoy this second stage for all it is.

Stage Two of your financial life is the quality-of-life stage, but nobody is going to just hand it to you. You have to go out there and build it for yourself.

CHAPTER SEVEN

RETIREMENT—STAGE THREE OF YOUR FINANCIAL LIFE

I don't think too much about retirement. There are a few reasons for that. The first is that I love working. I don't know if I will ever want to retire. I may want to add value to the McDonald's organization in different ways than I do today. Perhaps I will work three days a week coaching and mentoring up-and-coming managers and consultants. Or maybe there are other ways I can serve the organization when I no longer want to work full-time. But retire? No, thanks. The second reason I don't think too much about retirement is because I have been diligent in my retirement planning.

It would seem to me that the people who spend the most time thinking about retirement are those who don't like their jobs and those who have not adequately planned and prepared financially for retirement.

However, we all need to spend a little more time thinking about retirement in a very different way. This chapter is about that. You see, in truth, if you follow the plan outlined for Stage One of your financial life, you will not have to think much about retirement in terms of finances—no more than a couple of times a year. When your friends and colleagues start wondering and worrying in their forties and fifties about whether or not they will have enough money to retire, you will be pondering a much more exciting and elevated question—"What will I do with my time and my money when I retire?"—because you will have plenty of both.

Aren't You Glad?

In the coming years a growing number of people are going to become obsessed with worrying about whether Social Security will go bankrupt, whether they will outlive their money, and how rising taxes on consumption affect them as fixed income participants in the economy. But not you!

If you follow Option Two in Chapter 5, you will have saved approximately $61,000 by the time you are twenty-five years old. The day you retire (if you invested that $61,000 as outlined), you will be sitting on a nest egg of just over $2.7 million. Keep in mind this does not include any savings and investing you might have done after the age of twenty-five. It does not take into account any Social Security payments you might receive. It doesn't even take into account your 401(k), which I suggest you participate in at a minimum to take full advantage of your company's matching plan.

Aren't you glad you started early?

You could place the entire $2.7 million in triple tax-free municipal bonds (you want to learn more about those). In everyday language that means your $2.7 million would produce an annual income of approximately $138,000 tax-free forever without anyone ever touching the principal, using 5 percent as a rate guide.

Let me ask the question again: Aren't you glad you started early?

Stage Three—The Plan

In terms of finances, the plan here in Stage Three is very simple: Live off the income from your investments. As always, you have options. The other option is to consume the income from your investments and a part of your principal. Let me walk you through both options.

RETIREMENT OPTION ONE: LIVE OFF YOUR INVESTMENT INCOME

Let me paint a scenario for you. Imagine you followed Option Two in the right now stage and invested as outlined previously. Upon retirement you have more than $2.7 million in that account. Now let us also bring into play your 401(k) (which we have not even considered until now). Let's assume that you contributed $200 a month and received $200 a month in matching funds from the age of twenty-five to retirement at sixty-five. This account would now be worth $2,529,632. The numbers are really starting to add up, aren't they?

Right Now Savings Plan: $3,000,000
401(k) Plan: $2,529,632

Total Investable Assets
for Retirement: **$5,529,632**

It doesn't matter which way you look at it—it's a big number! Will it be easy to achieve? No. But is it possible? Yes, absolutely. And you can get there whether you work for McDonald's, own your own business, or have your dream job anywhere.

And let's not forget that since Stage One, you have not really denied yourself much. Sure you have contributed $200 a month to your 401(k) account. But these are stable numbers. Each year you earn more and the $200 becomes easier and easier to save.

So what do these numbers mean for your retirement? Well, Option One would be to simply live off the income from your investable assets. Historically the markets produce much more, but let's assume a return of just 5 percent during your retirement years. In the above example, with a return of 5 percent, you would have $276,481 each year to live on, and would likely never touch the principal. In fact, the principal would very likely continue to grow because you would be earning more than 5 percent and you would die with more than $6 million worth of financial legacy to empower future generations to do good.

RETIREMENT OPTION TWO:
DIE WITHOUT A PENNY

Perhaps you don't want to leave millions of dollars to your children or your favorite charity. Maybe you want to give it to them while you are still alive, or maybe you want to spend the money yourself and let them find their own way in life. Whichever may be the case, assuming the same numbers and conditions as Retirement Option One, and assuming that you live until eighty-five years of age (eight years above the average), then you would have to spend or give away almost $550,000 a year . . . every year . . . for twenty years . . . and you still might fail to die with nothing.

In both options, keep in mind that you probably don't have any debt at this point in your life. You are probably very happy with your home. You may want to do some minor renovations, but all of life's great expenses are behind you. Whether you choose Option One or Option Two, and whether it's $270,000 or $550,000 to spend each year, it is a lot of money.

Think about all the major expenses you have right now. They will probably no longer exist by the time you get to retirement. If you need a car, you will pay cash; you won't have a mortgage; and your children will likely have graduated or be about to graduate from college.

I can't help myself. Let me ask the question one more time: Aren't you glad you started early?

Playing Catch-up

I know. I make it sound so easy. There must be a catch. If it were this easy, more people would do it. Here's the thing. Most people don't start thinking about it early enough. They don't teach us about personal finances at school, not even in business school. How, and where, and from whom, are we supposed to pick it up? Are we just going to acquire it by osmosis? Certainly not from the current culture of ultra-consumption. If we are going to acquire anything by osmosis in this culture, it will be a financially life-threatening dose of overconsumption mixed with a financially paralyzing dose of consumer debt.

It is also important to note that while the numbers on the page look easy, those eight years of the right now stage, when you are first making money, you are saving diligently. That is not easy. Your friends will be buying stuff every time you turn around. A little voice inside you will be saying, "You deserve it," as you walk past stores. Succeeding with this stage is possible, but not easy, and the earlier you start, the better your chances are.

Now the rest of your friends and colleagues will spend their whole lives playing catch-up . . . and will fail, to varying degrees. Not because they are bad people. Best case scenario, nobody ever explained it to them or gave them a book like this. Worst case scenario, they knew what to do but lacked the discipline to set out on this path when they were young. That's a narrow window, but the difference is enormous.

Reflect on the almost $6 million you have for retirement

in the examples above. Now suppose somebody wakes up when they are thirty-five and decides to get serious about retirement savings. In order to reach $6 million by retirement (assuming all the same conditions we have assumed throughout the book regarding returns, etc.), he would have to save $2,725 a month, or almost $33,000 a year, for thirty years.

If someone didn't get serious about it until she was forty, just five more years, she would need to save $4,650 a month for twenty-five years to accumulate comparable retirement assets.

In each of these cases you need to remember that these people are also trying to save during the most expensive stage of their financial lives. Their expenses will never be higher than they are at this time when they come to the realization that they are not adequately preparing for retirement. Stage Two will also be the most expensive stage of your financial life, but you prepared for this reality by saving for retirement in Stage One. Now you can spend everything you earn in Stage Two and not have to worry. They cannot. They will feel themselves caught between the competing pressures of trying to save for retirement, enjoying all the good things that come with this stage of life, and providing for the needs and wants of their families. This pressure can be vise-like and can bring about broken relationships and great personal despair.

Before we move on, let us imagine that someone waited until he was fifty to begin getting serious about funding his retirement. You may think that it would not happen, but it happens much more often than you think. This person would have to save just shy of $15,000 a month to reach a comparable retirement to the one you set yourself up for in Stage One of your financial life.

The longer you wait, the harder it gets. Some people with enormous incomes wake up late and end up scraping by. They downsize, trim their spending, and watch their pennies. But in setting about to write this book, I did not have those people in mind. I had in mind very ordinary people like myself and my friends and colleagues who work at McDonald's. I had in mind the thousands of ordinary, hardworking people who come into our stores every day for lunch and a break from their work. And in these cases, it would simply be impossible to catch up from a late start.

This is how Warren Buffett, the best investor the world has ever known, expressed it: "It is better to start a little early and have the help of momentum, than to start late and be playing catch-up for the rest of your life."

Beyond the Money

The best things money affords us are freedom and opportunities. Once you know you don't have to worry about money in retirement, or in any stage of your life for that matter, you start to focus on the more important things. Money is not the most important thing if you have some. If you don't have enough money to pay your bills and feed your family, money becomes the most important thing.

Now that we have the money part of retirement out of

the way, we can move on to the more important aspects of retirement.

Those who work in the financial services industry talk about having a number. The number refers to the amount of money you would need to feel comfortable financially for the rest of your life. The amount of money you would need to walk away from whatever it is you are doing and never look back. On Wall Street, traders are notorious for two things: having ridiculously high numbers and revising those numbers once they actually reach them.

It would seem to me that the more important question is not "What's your number?" but rather "What are you going to do with your number when you get it?" This is the quintessential retirement question.

Let's face it, having money just for the sake of having money is absurd. Peter Thornhill, the Australian investment strategist, suggests this with startling clarity in his book *Motivated Money:* "Making money without having a dream to fulfill is pointless and obscene."

You are also much more likely to reach your number if you know exactly what it is you want to do with it once you get it.

A Vision for Retirement

When I ask people what they most look forward to about retirement, I get a broad range of answers. Certainly for some people it is the endless games of golf or the fantasy of not having to do anything, but this has become a less popular vision for retirement in more recent years. These are just some of the answers I have heard in the past couple of weeks:

- Spend more time with my children and grandchildren
- Write a book
- Walk the Appalachian Trail
- Volunteer at an inner-city school
- Travel in style
- Go back to school
- Get involved in a local theater group

You don't go back to school after you retire to improve your résumé or increase your income, you do it because you love learning. You don't join a theater group in retirement thinking you are going to become a movie star, you do it for the sheer pleasure of doing it. And you don't volunteer at an inner-city school for any other reasons than a desire to give back, to make a contribution, and the joy of being the difference that makes the difference.

The lesson we can learn from those who retire and do these things is that we should do a little more of these things in Stage Two, the quality-of-life stage. Hobbies, interests, and opportunities to give without receiving in return are essential to a person's happiness.

It may be convenient to say, "I don't have time for these things right now!" in Stages One and Two, but in truth, many of our best ideas come from these times. The reason innovation rarely comes from within existing organizations, or from the people in those organizations who are responsible for innovation, is because they get too close to it. We all get too close to our lives and careers from time to time, which is why we all need to step back from who we are, where we are, and what we are doing occasionally—and take another look.

Take a break once in a while. Play a round of golf or visit some folks in a nursing home who get no visitors. Your most innovative and creative ideas will come when you do.

Unique Opportunities

The one point I want to make abundantly clear as we think about retirement is this: Do something with your retirement years that only you can do. The more you tap into your unique talents and abilities, the more engaged you will stay. And personal engagement leads to a happiness that money simply cannot buy.

What I mean is, I don't want to see you taking a job at Wal-Mart as a greeter just to stay active or busy. That would be a waste. Follow the plan set out in this book and you won't need the money, so do something that allows you to make a unique contribution. If nothing else, volunteer for one of the countless nonprofit organizations trying to make your neighborhood, country, or world a better place. Don't take a paying job from someone else who will likely need it. Do something that no one else can do.

Some people are uniquely suited to doing specific things because they have certain talents or experience. Other people are uniquely suited to doing something because they do not need to be paid to do it. You will have both. When these two come together, a powerful opportunity to make a unique contribution emerges.

It says in Proverbs, "Where there is no vision, the people will perish" (28:19). We need a vision for our personal finances, and we need a vision for our career. We need a vision for our marriage, and we need a vision for parenting. We need a vision for our health and well-being, and we need a vision for our team. Schools need a vision, companies need a vision, churches need a vision, and countries need a vision. And in each instance, if there is no vision, the people will perish.

We also need a vision for retirement. It is amazing how many people die within a year or two of retirement. Many had no vision for this time. It is also amazing how many despise retirement once they get there. They also had no vision for retirement. So, whether you are sixteen or sixty, give some thought to how you want to spend this time of life we call retirement.

Just as it is never too early to start saving for those years, it is never too early to start thinking about what you want to do during them. Many people today live half their adult life in retirement. We are living longer. In 1935, when President Roosevelt signed the Social Security Act into law, the average life expectancy of an American was fifty-eight for a man and sixty-two for a woman. Today, we live on average almost twenty years longer. From a financial perspective, this is one of the reasons Social Security is bankrupt. In 1930 the great majority of people would pay into Social Security their whole lives and never draw on its benefits—as few lived to the age when benefits would commence. Today, the great majority live to the age when benefits begin, and well beyond.

By the time you retire, you are going to be able to live longer still and stay more active in the process. Many of your best years will be spent in retirement, so start formulating a vision for how you will spend your time and energy during those years.

CHAPTER EIGHT

LEGACY—STAGE FOUR OF YOUR FINANCIAL LIFE

The fourth stage of your financial life is all about building and leaving a legacy. Legacy is important, but as with so many things, it is the process not the end result that holds the real value. Building a legacy forces us to think about how we live our lives. This leads to a more proactive approach to life and more meaningful living. The legacy is a secondary positive outcome.

There are many kinds of legacy. You may want to raise your children to have a healthy sense of self. You may want to invent a product or process that revolutionizes your industry. You may want to preserve your family home. You may want to do your part to preserve the environment. You may want to leave a legacy of love. You may want to leave each of your children a large sum of money.

Our legacy is deeply personal and unique. It is a combination of many things. Your legacy may include some of the above, but not include the rest. There are parts to your legacy that I have never thought of because they are unique just to you.

Stage Four of your financial life is about building a legacy and leaving a legacy. While I acknowledge that there are many types of legacy, we will focus primarily here on the financial legacy that this book has taught you to create.

You Are Going to Die

It is never popular to talk about, but it is the one certainty for each and every one of us. One day this life as we know it is going to come to an end. On that day you are going to have a lot of money, and the question becomes what to do with it.

You may be tempted to think, "Well, if I am going to die with a lot of money, why should I save so hard?" The reason is because, as with many things in this world, there is no middle ground. People are either saving, investing, and accumulating wealth, or they are living from paycheck to paycheck burdened with consumer debt. You may also be tempted to think that some people can find the balance in between, but I assure you it is a precarious tightrope to walk.

Nonetheless, if you have come this far, I am going to assume that you have decided to take seriously the path I am laying before you. If that is indeed the case, you are going to die with a lot of money (or give away a lot of money toward the end of your life), and it is never too early to start thinking about this financial legacy.

In his "The Gospel of Wealth," Andrew Carnegie writes,

"To die rich is a disgrace." In recent times we have seen the wealthiest men of our age begin to divest themselves of their wealth in their later years, most notably Bill Gates and Warren Buffett.

Money—A Force for Good or Evil

It is impossible to ignore the power, emotion, and energy that money holds. It is because of these that money is either a force for good or a force for evil. Money is never neutral.

It is my hope that you will use the wealth I am teaching you to create throughout this book as a monumental force for good. What good will your wealth create? What good will your wealth bring about for yourself, your family, future generations, and people you have never met?

Let us turn to the first habit in Stephen Covey's book *The 7 Habits of Highly Effective People*—"Begin with the end in mind." What great thing would you do if you had a million dollars to give away this year? How would it change if you had $10 million or $100 million? There is no point accumulating the money if you don't have a dream to put it toward, and toward the end of your life that will mean a legacy dream.

Most people have plenty of dreams and no money to put toward them. Others have plenty of money and no dream to put the money toward. I'm not sure which is worse, but I suspect it is the latter.

Most people's legacy falls into two categories. The first is inheritance and the second is causes. Let us consider both.

INHERITANCE

Believe it or not, one of the great evils in this life is inherited wealth. Few events have the propensity to ruin a person's life like inheriting a fortune. There are many reasons, but the truth is that inheritance tends to create a sense of entitlement rather than empowerment and very often robs us of our drive to follow our own path, wherever it may lie.

The other reason inherited wealth can be so dangerous to a person's development is because the accumulation of wealth is usually accompanied by trials and tribulations that build character. You can give the money away, but you cannot as easily give the character away.

Finally, as obvious as it may seem, those who do not earn money almost never really appreciate how difficult it was to create the wealth in the first place.

Passing wealth on to the next generation therefore becomes something that requires a great deal of effort and planning.

A large part of my drive for financial success has been to change the financial DNA of my family forever. My father grew up in London, in the deepest kind of poverty imaginable. In one generation he was able to radically alter the financial destiny of our family. His path was more difficult than my path. He had to forge opportunities out of nothing, while I have had many opportunities placed before me for the taking.

I am not much interested in driving the latest BMW or wearing watches that cost more than most people spend on a car. Don't get me wrong, I like nice things, I enjoy the finer things in life, I hope to enjoy them more and more, and I never begrudge anyone these things. But what drives me in my quest to build and sustain wealth is my desire to set up future generations of my family to live incredible lives and do amazing things with the wealth we will build.

In most cases it will fall to our children to manage and disperse the future wealth of the family. With this in mind, it is critical to teach them about money. They will not learn about money and personal finances in high school, they will not learn about it in college, and they could even pass through business school and miss out on this vital aspect of any education.

Teaching our children about money means informing them about all the things we have explored in this book; it means making sure they are clear about their financial dreams, and, most of all, it means helping them to realize the tremendous power for good that money holds.

Most people I have discussed this topic with agree that education is one of the best, if not *the* best, form of inheritance. This in turn should broaden your children and grandchildren's minds sufficiently to help them find their own path in life. Which will in turn allow them to provide for themselves financially. Few people are ever truly happy spending someone else's money.

If your money stops your children and grandchildren from finding their own path in life, this would be a tragedy. Giving them everything they want and unlimited financial resources will almost certainly bring about this tragedy.

One couple I spoke with has dealt with this scenario by allowing their children to draw $1 from their trust for every dollar they earn. The limitation of this approach may be that their children will seek a high-paying job just to access more and more of their trust, rather than pursuing what they are genuinely passionate about in a way they feel they could really make a contribution.

Another couple I visited this topic with said that they always told their children, "You will always have enough money for what you need. We will make sure of that. So do what you feel called to do. Go out and make a difference in the world." This couple has a net worth of more than $20 million, and when I asked them what had promoted this part of their financial philosophy, they told me that they felt it was a great waste for the children of the wealthy to become accountants. I pressed a little more, asking why. They said that anyone can become an accountant, but everyone should take advantage of his or her unique talents and unique opportunities. In the case of the children of the wealthy, one unique opportunity is not necessarily having to do something that pays the bills.

Mary, the mother, explained further: "I have not had to work since my children were born. This unique opportunity has allowed me to use my abilities in unpaid situations—volunteering at school and at church, chairing various charitable committees. Someone who was working full-time would not be able to do all I have done in these arenas."

So there are many different approaches to how much money to pass on to your children and grandchildren, and how and when to do it, but everyone seems to agree with Warren Buffett on this point: "I wanted my children to be able to do anything they wanted, but I didn't want them to be able to do nothing."

Setting up the next generation means much more than giving them money. It means setting them up to be successful with money and investing, yes, but also teaching them to pursue fulfilling careers, meaningful relationships, health and well being, and most of all, the path that is theirs and theirs alone.

The money you saved in Stage One should be able to march on forever, essentially untouched, gaining size and momentum until your family becomes one of the great forces for good in the world.

Causes—The Sexy and the Not So Sexy

Everyone wants to feed the hungry children in Africa. It is what I call a sexy cause. Sexy not because of the work involved, but because of the conversation it makes for at cocktail parties. But nobody wants to build roads in Africa. Why? Infrastructure is not sexy. It doesn't make for good social conversation. As a result, much of the food we send for the starving people in Africa often rots on the docks, because they lack the roads and railways to get the food from port to the people.

There are 2 billion people on the planet today hungry just for bread. Here, now, in the twenty-first century, on our watch. In Africa alone, fifty thousand people die every day from extreme poverty and preventable disease. At the same time, and I realize it will be unpopular to say because it is one of the sexiest causes of our time, we seem obsessed with finding a cure for cancer, to the tune of tens of billions of dollars a year.

It may seem silly, or old-fashioned, but isn't there some natural order that suggests children dying of starvation deserve our more immediate attention than others dying late in life from advanced disease?

Nonetheless, with great wealth comes the possibility for a legacy cause (or causes) beyond the enrichment of future generations of our own family.

I have watched many families fail miserably in this area, but there is one success story that I find inspiring and noteworthy. I think we can all learn something from this example, regardless of how much or how little we have.

For the sake of anonymity let us call this family the Joneses. Bill and Mary Jones are parents to four children and have thirteen grandchildren. They have established a family foundation to manage the distribution of a large part of their wealth during and beyond their lives. The family foundation is separate from the trust they have set up to provide for their children, grandchildren, and future generations of their family.

The Jones family meets twice a year for what they call a family meeting. They discuss many aspects of family life during this meeting, which takes place in a rather formal, businesslike manner. The meeting usually lasts for two full days. One aspect of family life addressed is the distribution of funds from the Jones Family Foundation.

Established more than twenty years ago, the foundation

has earned a return of just over 9 percent on average. From the beginning Bill and Mary determined that they would distribute 5 percent of the funds each year. Bill's favorite causes are the college and high school he attended. Mary's favorite causes are their church and organizations working with young people to help them live more meaningful lives, to discover their mission in life. They each distributed $250,000 to charitable causes last year.

Bill and Mary's four adult children are entitled to distribute $100,000 each per year to charities of their choosing. But in order to do so they must comply with the following. They must be personally involved with any charity that they distribute more than $5,000 to, and they must make a presentation once a year to the whole family meeting about the charities they are supporting and why. As part of these presentations, they submit a request for the amount of funding they would like to give to different charities the following year. Based on their presentation, the family then votes to approve or decline the distribution.

Each of Bill and Mary's grandchildren over the age of twelve is able to distribute $2,000, those grandchildren above the age of sixteen distribute $10,000, and those above the age of twenty-one distribute $25,000.

I am sure the process is not perfect, but as you can see, Bill and Mary have done a lot of thinking and planning to bring it about. It is the best example of thoughtful financial planning I have seen, and I am sure it is better than not having a plan or process at all.

The Joneses' process allows future generations to learn

slowly how to give money away. It also provides a forum for Bill and Mary to talk about why they support the charities they do, thus giving their children and grandchildren valuable insight into their values—the values that allowed them to build the wealth in the first place.

Educate Your Children (and Grandchildren) About Money

This leads us right into an area of multigenerational wealth that is ignored in a staggeringly high number of cases—educating children and grandchildren about money.

The wealthy are notorious for neglecting to teach their children about money. Surprisingly, the worst—in my experience—tend to be those who are in financial fields such as accounting, investment advising, and banking.

When it comes to educating children and grandchildren about money, those who have done so successfully all say the same thing: Start early.

Your children and grandchildren do not need PhDs in money management, but they do need the basics: They should be well versed in the laws of money as outlined on page 26, and they need to be aware that when we say yes to one thing we are doing so at the cost of other things—that is, we are always allocating scarce resources.

Ninety percent of lottery winners have less money after ten years than they had before they won the lottery. Unless you educate your children and grandchildren about money, whatever money you leave them will be like winning the lottery, and they will almost certainly waste it.

Focus Your Legacy

Most of the world tuned in a couple of years ago when Warren Buffett gave away more than $40 billion, almost his entire fortune. But every day very ordinary people leave fortunes to their favorite causes.

In 1998, Mildred Othmer died in her Brooklyn home where she had lived for decades with her husband. Three years earlier he had died. They lived a very ordinary life in a very ordinary neighborhood. They didn't drive fancy cars, take exotic holidays, or wear designer label clothes.

Both Mildred and her husband Donald dedicated their whole careers to education, he as a college professor and she as a schoolteacher.

Don and Mildred Othmer were described by friends and neighbors as having lived comfortably and modestly. So you can imagine their surprise when they learned that Donald and Mildred left behind assets of more than $800 million, all of which was left to charity and most of which was left to colleges and universities.

What Buffett, Mr. and Mrs. Othmer, and most successful philanthropists have in common is that they focused their giving, and thus their legacy.

Spread your legacy too thin and you will render it ineffective, no matter how much money you leave.

Find something you are passionate about and focus your legacy on that cause, issue, or need.

Generosity

Whatever form yours takes, legacy is about generosity. It is about being generous with our time, talent, and treasure. It's about giving back to the community or society at large for all the opportunities we have enjoyed because of the generosity of countless men and woman who have gone before us.

The thing with generosity is that you don't wake up all of a sudden one day and decide to be generous. Generosity is something that is deeply ingrained in our character, or not at all. In accumulating wealth, it is easy to get so caught up in the accumulating that you forget to be generous.

My experience has led me to believe that the people who were generous before they had great fortunes are still generous after they have great fortunes. Those who refuse to be generous before they are wealthy tend to remain miserly after they are wealthy. Money doesn't change people—it just magnifies who we really are.

Recently I was helping to raise money for a local charity and I called on a family friend who has a net worth of between $20 and $30 million dollars. He has always claimed to love the cause and said that he believes it is important work, and every year he sends a check for $500. But this year the committee was asking him to make a gift of $5,000. He turned me down cold. He said, and I quote, "When it comes to charities, I am more of a $500 man." He is seventy years old and will die with millions and millions of dollars, but he cannot let go of his scarcity mentality.

The next week I received a check for $1,000 for the same

charity from a schoolteacher who works in a poor inner-city school and makes about $30,000 a year.

Be generous. Whether you have $10 million today or don't have $100 in your bank account, decide from the outset to be generous. First in small ways, but over time in increasingly larger ways. Compete with yourself to be more generous with every passing year.

Enough Is Enough

Sooner or later we all realize that enough is enough. The wisest people seem to recognize that happiness does not come from having more things and more money, but from the satisfaction of a life well spent. In preparing to write this book, I interviewed dozens of people of all ages. One of the themes that emerged with the older interviewees was the idea that the older you get, the less money you spend. They also affirmed that they were happiest in their lives when they were focused on what they really needed, rather than what they selfishly wanted. They also said that a lifestyle that considers the whole person makes for the most fulfilling life.

The great majority of those who have amassed fortunes rarely get caught up in the hype of wealth. They are more interested in the simple things in life and realize that they need very little. Over and over, from dozens of people I spoke with, I was quoted the words "He who needs the least has the most."

It was interesting that many of the people with this attitude thought it was inevitable that they would become wealthy and leave an enormous financial legacy behind. When I asked them about this posture of confidence, they explained that most of what we spend money on we don't really need. We tend to spend the great majority of our income on superficial things, extra things, and upgrading everything.

Interviewing dozens of men and women about their financial legacies has inspired me more than ever to think about my own. When I think of the legacy I would like to leave behind when I leave this world, there are five components that come to mind.

First, I want my family and friends to know that I love them, that I have done what I could to support them in their efforts to live their dreams, and that I am grateful for the ways they have helped me live my dreams.

The second component of my legacy as I imagine it today is what we have spent most of this book discussing. If I did not save another penny for the rest of my life, and invested my net worth in the ways I have encouraged you to throughout this book, I would leave a financial legacy of at least $20 million. I have arranged these assets in such a way that my children will not be able to dilute them; thus they will pass on to my grandchildren more than $1 billion. This legacy is already created. I have done the hard work. Barring any catastrophe or the undoing of my legal wishes, this legacy will live on for hundreds of years and will likely continue to gather momentum with every generation.

The third component of my legacy is the education of my children about life and money. They will be guardians of this fortune. If I teach them as I hope to about life and money, they will not need this money for themselves. I am not opposed to them accessing some of it for their educations and other legitimate needs, but I do not want this family fortune to become a disincentive to any generation in the future.

You are experiencing part of the fourth component of my legacy right now. It was only a few months after I began my journey toward financial freedom that I decided that I wanted to help other people along this path also. I was continually amazed how financially illiterate most people around me were, and I wanted to do something about that. It is now more than ten years later and this book is the first step in that effort. One of my dreams is that 1 million people will put what I have shared in this book into action. If they follow Option Two set out for Stage One, they will each leave approximately $12.2 million (if on average they die at eighty). If the next generation has the discipline to keep this money invested, they will pass on around $600 million. The next generation will pass on $25 billion. That's billion, with a B. So if only forty people take what I have written in these pages to heart and really apply it, this book will have a trillion-dollar legacy. I hope it is more than forty people who put this system to work, and I hope you are one of them.

The fifth and final component of my legacy I must admit I am not at all sure about yet. I know that my plan will produce an income far greater than future generations of my family could ever spend. With that in mind, I am always pondering what focus we should bring to our family legacy when it comes to charitable work. At thirty-one, I hope I have a few more years to work this out, but at this time I am leaning toward using part of my financial legacy to combat financial illiteracy. It baffles me that millions of so-called educated people know so little about managing their personal finances.

The bottom line when it comes to the legacy stage is this: You are going to accumulate a tremendous fortune during your lifetime. You are going to die. You cannot take it with you. Thus, you are going to leave a tremendous financial legacy behind. Start thinking about what incredible good you want that financial legacy to achieve.

CHAPTER NINE

MY FUTURE, YOUR FUTURE, AND THE FUTURE OF McDONALD'S

Everything great in history has been built by people who believed that the future could be bigger than the past. My parents always encouraged me to dream of good things for my future, and challenged me not to be put off by the first obstacle that got between me and my dreams. If you study the history of McDonald's as a company, you will find that what it is today was built by thousands of people who dreamed of a bigger future. McDonald's has faced enormous challenges throughout its history, but every generation of owner operators, corporate executives, and employees has found ways to turn those challenges into opportunities. It is my hope that this book has convinced you that your future can be bigger than your past, and not only in a financial sense, but in every area of your life.

The Future of McDonald's

Throughout the history of McDonald's there have always been naysayers. At the beginning they said fast food was a fad that would not last, and that McDonald's would not succeed, and I expect that the voice of these naysayers will always be with us. But McDonald's presses on to a bigger and better future every year for its customers, employees, and shareholders.

If you had invested $1,000 in McDonald's shares in 1989, twenty years later, in 2009, your investment would have been worth $7,813.13. That's an increase of 681 percent.

There are many reasons that McDonald's continues to be successful decade after decade, but here I would like to focus on three aspects of the company's success that are essential to your future and mine.

INNOVATION AND IDEAS

The first is the McDonald's approach to innovation. Most large companies have whole departments of people that are responsible for innovation, or huge research and development departments that are very insular. McDonald's is committed in each of these areas, but the culture since the beginning has been one that is open to the best ideas regardless of where they come from. If a brilliant idea comes from someone whose job it is to innovate and come up with new ideas—great. But if the brilliant idea comes from an owner operator with no background in innovation and no advanced degree, that's just as good. Ideas are judged on their merits, not on their source.

In fact, many of the anchors of our menus today were developed by owner operators. Here are just a few examples:

1963—Filet-O-Fish developed by owner operator Lou
    Groen
1966—Hot Apple Pie developed by owner operator Litton
    Cochrane
1967—Big Mac developed by owner operator Jim Delligatti
1971—Egg McMuffin developed by owner operator Herb
    Peterson
1998—McFlurry Desserts developed by owner operator
    Ron McLellan

The best ideas almost never come from where you expect
them to come, and the best corporate cultures allow ideas to
emerge and blossom regardless of their source. McDonald's is
not just one good idea. It is sixty years of good ideas.

*Your future, my future, and the future of McDonald's depend on
our ability to stay open to good ideas regardless of their source.*

CONTINUOUS IMPROVEMENT

The second reason McDonald's success deserves special mention here is the company's commitment to continuous improvement.

In 1940, when the McDonald brothers opened their ham-
burger restaurant, they had no idea what they were giving
birth to. Like so many of us they were just trying to make a
living to support their families and build a bigger future.
Fourteen years later Ray Kroc visited the restaurant and had
his own vision of a bigger future—and the franchise system
was born. Every year since then a new product has been tested
or introduced. Some have stood the test of time and some

have not. Products that have failed inspired later products that would enjoy enormous success. In this way it is impossible to separate our failures from our successes. If we had not known what didn't work, we would not have been able to pinpoint exactly what would work.

While the genius of the systems makes the McDonald's business model so enviable, the business itself is constantly evolving into something new and better. Almost nothing remains untouched by our company's desire for continuous improvement. While to a casual observer our business remains the same, in reality our business is constantly being transformed at an alarming rate. What now seems like it has always been there, such a cultural icon as breakfast at McDonald's, is a very recent addition in the whole scheme of the business.

We have a way of introducing new and innovative products that in the blink of an eye people can't imagine they ever lived without.

The way we leverage technology is constantly advancing, and our systems are always being refined for maximum efficiency; our restaurants look nothing like they did twenty years ago, and twenty years from now will look completely different again. All this and we haven't mentioned a product. Every time the naysayers suggest that we have reached our limit, the combination of innovation, continuous improvement, and our people prove them wrong. They said our business could not grow any more, but then we introduced a breakfast menu, which revolutionized our business and the industry. They said we could not grow any more, but then we introduced McSalads and the lighter choice menu. They said we could not grow any more yet again, and now we are grabbing market share from Starbucks with our premium coffee.

And yet, in the midst of all this constant change, the Golden Arches remain one of the most recognized symbols in the world, and the promise of the McDonald's brand has never changed.

Your future, my future, and the future of McDonald's depend on our commitment to continuous improvement.

NOTHING WITHOUT PEOPLE

People are the core of everything we do at McDonald's. Our discussions about innovation and continuous improvement would be moot without the people who have given rise to both throughout the history of McDonald's. On any given day 1.5 million McDonald's employees are making it happen. Harnessing the energies and efforts of 1.5 million people is no easy task. After all, you know how difficult it is to get ten people together for lunch.

Ever since I showed an interest in having a career with McDonald's, the company has been investing in me. Over the years I have attended courses to improve my skills in the following areas: management, leadership, communication, business strategy, and many others. Beyond the formal training, it is amazing how much you learn on a daily basis because you are in the midst of a world-class business and the systems that drive it toward success.

Going forward, I see people as our biggest challenge. The increasing pressure to find, hire, nurture, and retain the best people is a threat to our bigger future, and our best ideas and efforts will be required to face this challenge. But I have no doubt that we will find a way to thrive amid this challenge and in the process will lead our industry to new ways of engaging their employees.

Your future, my future, and the future of McDonald's depend on our ability to attract, hire, nurture, develop, and retain a world-class workforce.

UNIVERSAL PRINCIPLES

I do not think these three drivers are unique to McDonald's. In fact, I believe they are universal principles and that you and I should be pursuing them as rigorously personally as McDonald's is pursuing them as a business. What happens to a person who is open to finding new ideas wherever they are to be found, who has an unwavering commitment to continuous improvement, and who is constantly developing him- or herself? That person's future will be bigger than the past. How many people do you actually know who pursue these three principles vigorously? These are the signs of a world-class business, a world-class employee or team, and a person whose future will be an amazing adventure.

My Future

I have made many sacrifices to be where I am today, and I can honestly say I am glad that I did. Here are just a few so that you can consider the path I have been willing to walk.

Until I was thirty, I did not have a car and used public

transport to get around. I cannot count the number of hours I have worked without pay in order to achieve incredible results and secure the next step in my career. I always worked as long as was necessary to finish my job. I have brushed aside every other business and employment opportunity that has been presented to me in fifteen years. I never turn my cell phone off. I always put the needs of my people in front of my own. I have treated the stores I manage and consult to as if they were my own business. I use my own money to reward and inspire employees. I have worked so many twenty-four-hour shifts I cannot count them. I have never asked for a pay raise. And I have never spent more than my weekly budget.

Learning to make sacrifices has produced in me habits and character that will hold me in good stead forever. My future is not dependant on what other people think of me, but on who I am as a person. Those for whom I have worked and those who have worked with me or for me know that I am the kind of person that makes things happen. When four years ago I took over the six stores I oversee, they were making a collective profit of just over $700,000. Today those same six stores are producing a collective profit of more than $2.8 million. People around me know that I may not be the smartest academically, but I am always improving, I am committed to my role and my people, and I love what I do.

I don't know what my future will hold. Like you, I do not have a crystal ball. The role I have at the moment is perfectly suited to me in many ways. There are higher positions that I know would not be so well suited to my unique abilities. I hope the leaders and managers that I support always try to place me where I can add the most value . . . and to this day, my results have spoken for themselves.

Needless to say, there is a whole world of opportunities outside of McDonald's, but in a time and place when many people will work for more than ten companies over the course of their careers, I hope I can retire from McDonald's. My career so far has been enjoyable and rewarding. There have been many hardships and heartaches, and plenty of challenges and opportunities for growth. I don't regret them or resent them. They have all made me who I am today.

The only thing I am certain of is that if I continue to apply all I have learned and shared with you in this book to my life and my career wherever I find myself, I will continue to add value . . . and that will result in an ever-bigger future.

Your Future

You are almost at the end of this book, but this is just the beginning of your financial journey. This book can completely change your life. Twenty years from now, if you take the ideas in these pages seriously, you will divide your life into two parts—before you read this book and after you read it. This will be a defining moment of your life if you decide to make it one.

By now your mind has no doubt suggested many reasons why you cannot follow this plan. These are just excuses. Some of them may be valid in a limited way, but all of them can be overcome. Again, if I can do it, I firmly believe that anyone who genuinely gives it his or her best effort and de-sires it can also do it.

In closing I will share with you what I believe is the core of our business success at McDonald's and the habit that will drive your financial success from this day on: Measure it. At McDonald's we measure everything. We measure food costs, transactions, hourly sales, daily sales, weekly sales, monthly sales, annual sales, cost of labor, total number of employee hours worked each day, shift, week, and month, sales per em-ployee hour, rent as a percentage of revenue, and hundreds of other things that would require technical explanation. We measure everything.

The reason we measure everything is because if you cannot measure it you cannot change it. There is no point in me say-ing to one of my managers or one of my crew members that we need to reduce our food waste and expecting that person to make it happen without a measurement. I need to say to that manager or crew member that last month our food waste (raw and completed waste) was 1 percent and this month we need to get that number back below 0.75 percent. Now that person is clear about my expectations and knows how I will measure the results, and success or failure is in his or her hands.

Once you have set your plan, created a budget, and started along the path to financial freedom, I want to encourage you to start measuring your financial progress the way we mea-sure everything in our business at McDonald's.

When I first became a manager, I was responsible for measuring all these things, but particularly hourly, daily, and weekly revenue and expenses. I started to think to myself, "If everyone managed their personal income and expenses the way I do for this store, everyone's financial situation would be very different." So I started to manage my personal finances in the way I was managing the store finances.

This is what I would like to encourage you to do on an ongoing basis for the rest of your life, if you want to succeed in the path I have laid before you in these pages:

1. Always stay clear about your goals.
2. Track your expenses and income on a monthly basis. In the beginning you may want to do this weekly so that you monitor your changing habits and ensure success.
3. Read one book each month about personal finances. If you are a slow reader like me, get the audio edition and listen on the way to work or while you are working out.

These three habits will keep all that we have discussed in this book fresh and present in your mind, which in turn will affect your actions, which in turn will create new habits, which in turn will build character—and your character is your destiny.

Your Own Financial System

The key to McDonald's success is the systems and processes that drive the daily behaviors of the 1.5 million employees around the world. When managers and owner operators stick to the systems, they find success. When they don't stick to the systems, they almost always fail. The same is true for financial success. You need systems and processes that will automatically lead you to be financially successful. These are what I have tried to summarize for you in this book.

So now you have a system for financial success. Study the system. Follow the system. Review the system. If you stick to the system, I am confident that you will live an incredibly rich and rewarding life. The disciplines you will learn by applying this system to your finances will lead to incredible wealth, but these disciplines will also lead to fulfillment in your relationships, and in the areas of health and well being, and will become the foundation of success in whatever you choose to pursue in your life.